Escape to Prosperity

Wes Beavis

D0051289

POWERBORN

Los Angeles ◆ Sydney

Escape to Prosperity
by Wes Beavis

Copyright ©1999 W. J. Beavis

7th printing June 2000

PRINTED IN THE UNITED STATES OF AMERICA BY
KNI Inc.

COVER & ILLUSTRATIONS BY
Joe VanSeveren

COPYRIGHT & PUBLISHING ADMINISTRATION

POWERBORN
631 Via Paraiso
Corona, California USA 92882
Phone (909)739-0634
Fax (413)825-8137
www.WesBeavis.com

Beavis, Wesley James, 1962-
    Escape to Prosperity/ Wes Beavis
        p.   cm.
    ISBN 1–888741–02–3
    1. Success in business—United States.   2. Quality of life—
United States.   3. Work & Family—United States.
    4. Self-actualization / Maturation (Psychology)   I. Title
        158.1 BEA —dc20   1999
    Library of Congress Catalog Card Number 98-68200

Dedicated to the ones who planted the seeds of love, faith and adventure in me. . . my parents, David and Elaine.

Special Thanks

To the owners of the Desert Diamond for providing me a floating home in paradise to write this book.

To Dr. and Mrs. Smith for the mountain top inspiration.

To the people who gave me counsel and wisdom regarding this subject.

To all the leaders who, over the years, have invited me to speak and perform for their people.

Your generosity attests to your prosperity.

Contents

Escape from. . .

Escape to

prosperity (pro sper´i tē) **n.** [< L. *prosperus*, favorable] thriving condition, success, wealth, continuous state of well being, etc.

Introduction

The other night, my wife and I drove into the city for a dinner appointment. We knew our destination but our directions for how to get there were vague. We finally arrived almost an hour late and somewhat exhausted from navigating the unknown territory. Not having clear directions made the trip harder than it needed to be.

This is what it is like for many people who want to be prosperous. They want prosperity but for a lack of clear directions they have a hard time finding where it is located. Some people, frustrated by the challenges of life, give up on the notion that prosperity will ever be their experience. They resign themselves to a life of always struggling, all the while thinking, "I must not have been meant for the good life."

The reality is that we are made for the good life. Some of us just get lost in things which prevent us from finding the good life.

Some time ago while I was out walking, my mind was consumed with this thought: *Why is life so difficult for many of my friends?* As I walked, I wondered why their lives were burdened with more struggles than celebrations. Why were they living with more restraints than freedoms? They seem trapped in a life of overcoming one difficulty just to face another. They are good people, I thought, so why are they not living with the prosperity that their goodness deserves? They work hard, they are dedicated to good causes and they genuinely want the best out of life. Then why are they not getting the best out of life? Why do they live under a cloud of stress?

The simple answer 'life is tough' was not a good enough explanation for me. Life being hard is a valid issue but my experience was telling me that it need not be that hard. There had to be more. I ended up walking for almost two hours while my mind searched for possible answers. My quest for answers continued in the months that followed. It motivated me to read every relevant book I could find, interview several significant people and evaluate my own experience. The bottom line was to find out if good people could experience a truly victorious life. To me that meant living a life with less struggle and more prosperity.

My journey of discovery, as you will find, has been a good one. I have encouraging news to report. It confirms what my experience has taught me. There is no reason why anyone should be at the mercy of life's hardships unnecessarily. It is possible to have a life with less struggle and more prosperity. And what is more, you don't need a satellite navigational system to get you there!

In preparation for the writing of this book, I floated my ideas with a friend who e-mailed this response: "Wes, I presume *Escape to Prosperity* will encourage people to achieve a large and positive balance in their 'quality of life account'—many of whom have their account in overdraft due to misguided and inappropriate pursuits in life."

My answer is YES. That is exactly what I want this book to do for people. Help them, regardless of their background, to become millionaires in their quality of life. Help them to have an abundance of the following:

- Self-fulfillment

- Financial Victory

- Personal Freedom

The prosperity principles of this book will work for anyone. Prosperity is not elusive. It is readily accessible to everyone who desires it enough. A life of freedom and abundance is what every person is meant to have. Not only that, but what you learn on your journey to prosperity ensures that you will never lose it.

Escape to Prosperity will help you to establish a thriving life of continual success and well being.

— Wes Beavis —

Chapter 1

Escape from a Life that
Resembles a Prison

As a youngster I remember my mother taking me to see the movie *Born Free*, the dramatic story of a lion cub that was separated from its mother at birth. It was rescued by a veterinarian and raised in captivity until it became obvious that this animal was not born to be caged. It was decided that this lion needed to be released from captivity and returned to the freedom of living in the wild.

I have yet to see the awesome sight of lions roaming freely across the African savannah. My only exposure to these majestic beasts has been at the courtesy of the various zoos of the world for which I am grateful. It's nice to observe lions in close proximity without the risk of becoming their next delicious snack. Yet, whenever I see a caged lion, my mind is always drawn to think, "Something is wrong with this picture."

The same can be said about people. When I see people living a life of captivity, caged by a low self-opinion, destructive habits and relationships, a boring job and a mountain of debt, again I think to myself, "Something is wrong with this picture!" We are simply not meant to live a life such as this.

We, too, are born free. We are free to explore, free to develop skills, free to imagine, free to succeed, and free to determine our destiny. But that is where it ends for most of us.

It is apparent that we are also free to trade in our freedom for other things. For instance, one of the biggest temptations of the modern world is the offer that you can 'have it now and pay for it later!' Wow! What a great deal. But you surely pay for it later. John Jefferson Davis once wrote: "A society like our own, which becomes preoccupied with the gratification of desires in the present, will inevitably find itself becoming impoverished in the future." And that is what has happened. Too many people are never going to find prosperity in their own lives because they have traded their future freedom for the sake of having things now.

Rarely do we lose our freedom in one transaction. It is the slow, subtle selling off that devastates us. A piece here and another piece there. When we finally add all the amounts, we discover more freedom has been traded than we intended.

It starts out with little trade-offs which we hardly notice. We don't mind because the things for which we trade our freedom promise us happiness. And true to the promise, we do experience happiness. But the happiness only lasts for a short while. Then we start looking for other things to make us happy and willingly trade a little more of our freedom to attain whatever that may be.

Consequently, after a few years of consistent trading, we realize that we have given up so much freedom that we now feel imprisoned in a life that is hard to escape. No longer are we as free as we once were to chart our own course through life. We have relinquished ourselves to the captivity of a lifestyle, a timetable, a boss, payment plans, financial institutions, and a myriad of other entities. People and things now lay claim to how we should spend our lives. The net result is that the things for which we traded our freedom, the very things that were meant to fulfill us, now serve to imprison us.

The answer for every person in this situation is simple: Stop transforming your life into a prison. You were born for prosperity not for captivity. A fulfilled life that is rich with personal freedom is the way we are meant to live. Any other form of existence is as inappropriate as the 'king of the jungle' being caged and urbanized.

Start Planning Your Escape

Are you struggling to feel like a lion because you are not enjoying the freedom of a lion? The solution has more to do with releasing you from captivity than sending you to classes on "How to Be a Lion." Are you feeling like you are not living in prosperity? The answer lies more with releasing you from the things that make you poor rather than teaching you how to 'get' prosperity. Prosperity is not something that needs to be chased. It is something that will inevitably come to you when you escape the things that make you poor.

It's time to break free from the things that impoverish you. Liberation is at hand! Get ready to escape to PROSPERITY.

Choose the Fun that Ends with Fun

"Feet, don't fail me now!" was my desperate plea as I tried to stomp out a fire that I had just created. It was the summer of 1975 and the beginning of school vacation. My best friend Jeff Morgan, my younger brother Chris and I had

15

ventured deep into the state forest that surrounded our home in Illinois. We had found a book of matches and knowing there were plenty of dry leaves on the ground from the previous fall, we devised a game.

With all the stupidity of which teenagers are sometimes capable, we started a little fire in the leaves. The game plan was to wait until the fire started to spread, then we would run over and stomp the fire out with our feet. Each time we successfully eradicated the fire, we would 'up the stakes' by letting the fire spread a little further to increase the challenge. It was the ultimate adrenaline rush. Time after time we were able to stomp the fire out of existence. We were having so much fun.

Little thought was given to what would happen if we lost the game. And lose the game we did. Using the very last match, we decided to let the fire burn longer than ever before. Then with all the fury of charging gladiators we attacked the fire as it rapidly spread beyond control. This time we knew that we had let it go too far. We stomped frantically but our flurry of activity seemed to just stir the flames all the more.

As the surrounding trees started to catch alight, we knew defeat was imminent. Looking at each other we realized that the name of the game had changed from having fun to saving our own skins. We ran for our bicycles and high-tailed it home. As we did, the sound of the town fire siren pierced the air both hailing the volunteer firemen from their places of work and signalling that we were in major trouble.

Jeff, Chris and I decided to rendezvous at my house so that we could assess the gravity of our situation. The smell of melted sneakers filled the bedroom. The stylish frayed hemlines of our jeans had burned off and the stench of charred leg hair reminded us that our dance partner could have killed us. My brother Chris had somehow singed his hair badly enough to elicit the interest of enquiring minds. Seeking to conceal the evidence and wanting to avoid the state of his hair being the cause of an interrogation, I decided to give him a haircut. My salon skills combined with some blunt school scissors did not leave us with the desired result.

The sound of blaring fire engine sirens with the intermittent voices of firemen over two-way radios could be heard from our front yard. With each passing moment, we knew we would not get away with this. So we decided to go to the police station and turn ourselves in.

We were detained until our parents, who at

the request of the chief of police, arrived at the police station. It was decided that criminal charges would not be filed providing we successfully completed a period of probation. It was also decided that punishment should be left to the discretion of our parents—a very smart move by the police chief. He knew that my father was a firm believer in the proverb: "Spare the rod and you'll spoil the child."

With wisdom and the help of a cheap imitation leather belt, Dad faithfully administered a good dose of tough love. Designed to deliver me from any pyromaniac tendencies, his effort was purposeful and swift. Receiving the message clearly, I promptly recommitted myself to a life of abstaining from acts of utter stupidity.

Afterwards, I received a dramatic lecture from my mother on the evils of playing with fire. Finally, to ensure that I would not prematurely forget the foolishness of my actions, they grounded me. All fun and social activities were cancelled for the whole summer. My younger brother Chris, though more an accomplice than an instigator in the perpetration, not only received the same punishment, but carried the added embarrassment of a really bad haircut.

This experience served to teach me that not all fun ends with fun. This principle is paramount to becoming prosperous. There is a lot of fun to be had in life. But if you want to have a life of prosperity, you must never choose fun that does not end with fun. Prosperous people examine their activities and decisions, and ensure that the consequences will only add to their prosperity. The best fun is that which lasts and lasts and has no penalty to pay to anyone at the end.

It bewilders me when people borrow money to go on a vacation. There is nothing more uninspiring than paying for a vacation that you have already had. Yet this is an example of how a lot of people are living their lives. They have already had the fun and now they are paying the price for it. All this does is contribute to the feeling that you are trapped, working for the benefit of everyone else except yourself, because you have already had your fun. It is a reversal of the way it should be.

Be Consequential in Your Approach to Fun

Those who evaluate fun in the light of its consequences end up having the most joy and freedom in life. There's nothing wrong with throwing oneself into the offer of a 'good time'.

But to do so without regard for where that experience may leave you is dangerous. Short-sightedness is the number one reason people find themselves serving a life rather than living a life.

I recently heard of a man who was perilously close to having an affair. Though the struggle was immense, he did not give in to the temptation. When asked what stopped him, he said, "When I felt that I was going to 'pass the point of no return', I pictured myself standing on the front porch of my house saying goodbye to my children and trying to explain to them why daddy would not be living with them anymore." He said that it was a strong enough picture to deter him from advancing into the arms of temptation. He did not say that the flirtations were not fun. Yet when he stopped to consider where this fun would lead, he realized that there would be an expensive penalty to pay later on for his actions. The consequences of this fun were not going to lead to more fun.

Napoleon Hill, the renowned author of *Think and Grow Rich*, once said: "If you want prosperity, you must refuse to accept any circumstances that lead toward poverty."

Become consequential in your thinking. Ask yourself, "What effect will this experience, relationship or purchase have on my future?"

Take Hill's advice and avoid situations which lead to impoverishment. Do not 'buy in' to anything that will cost your future happiness and freedom. Examine the 'opportunities' offered to you in the light of where the opportunity may leave you. Does the opportunity leave you richer or poorer in the long run?

Consequential thinking will help you to make the right decisions. Decisions which will lead to prosperity. The consequence of a good decision always adds and never takes away from your future joy.

Consequential thinking is the key to self-fulfillment, financial victory, and personal freedom. Making decisions that result in these things ensures the inevitability of our prosperity.

Self-fulfillment

Achieving a personally fulfilling life is the ultimate quest. There is nothing more satisfying than knowing you are living life to your greatest potential. The truly prosperous person is the one who can say "I love my life."

Yet as simple as it sounds, self-fulfillment eludes many people. Sometimes, in our quest, we engage in activities and thought processes which do not provide satisfying outcomes.

21

Instead of a life of prosperity, the consequences of our actions and thoughts enslave us. We are trapped by our low self-opinion, our imperfections and our bad habits.

Financial Victory

Clearly, money is a source of quicksand for many people. Money is so much fun to spend but many people are sinking into anxiety, despair and embarrassment because of their spending habits. The handling of money has the power to release you to freedom or to put you in the poorhouse. Sadly, for many, it is the latter.

A friend of mine says that there is nothing wrong with money except for the love of it and the lack of it. In all cases, whether it be loving it, lacking it, or overspending it, money ceases to be a blessing and becomes a burden. The key to having money bless you rather than burden you resides in making prosperity based decisions.

Personal Freedom

The currency of prosperity is freedom. Ultimately, the amount of say we have in what we do with our lives is the way prosperity is calculated. All the fancy trimmings in the world mean nothing if we are tied down to things which limit the exploration of our potential. No job, relationship, or situation in life is worthy of dictating the terms of our destiny.

Unfortunately, too many of us live confined and restricted lives. All too often, our lack of freedom is self-inflicted. We make decisions for immediate gratification. No regard is given to whether the decision will compliment or curse us in the long run.

Life is better lived with a generous supply of freedom. Your creative spirit is released when you have control over how you spend your day.

Make the Decision for Prosperity

The most significant force in determining whether we live in freedom or captivity is our minds. How we think determines how much prosperity we will experience. Prosperity starts with our decision to change the way we have been managing our lives and resources. For instance, your first step may be to resolve to no longer let the fun today be the culprit that steals the joy from life tomorrow.

We are designed for lifelong fun and freedom. The challenge is that we can be seduced into a lifestyle which is more about confinement than fun and freedom. If you are tired of living in captivity, it is no wonder. You were born to be free. It is what you are made to experience. Prosperity will be yours with every good decision that leads you out of captivity. Remember, when you escape the things that make you poor, prosperity will naturally flow to you.

Chapter 2

Escape from the Shackles of
Low Self-Opinion

If I could choose one human condition to put on trial for crimes against humanity, I would choose low self-opinion. It would be charged with the crimes of causing depression, dissension, divorce, debt, discouragement, degradation and these are just the crimes starting with the letter 'D'. In such a trial, it would be hard to find an impartial jury because everybody has been robbed by a low self-opinion at some time in their life. Even worse, some people invite this robber home to live with them. They end up feeding and caring for their low self-opinion. All the time this imposter is robbing them of prosperity.

Our performance and productivity reflects our self-image. Prosperity flows to us when we think positively of ourselves, our abilities, and our future. It is that simple.

Now begs the question: If a low self-opinion pays a pathetically low wage that only leads us to the poorhouse, why do we find ourselves shackled to one? Surely no one would embrace a low self-opinion on purpose. Nobody in their right mind sets out to sabotage their self-esteem but it still happens. Life provides for us ample traps upon which we can stumble. We never intend to be shackled to these traps but by the time we realize our ensnarement, they can be hard traps from which to break free.

Here are five classic traps that hamper people from moving forward.

Trap #1

I Want to Be Perfect

I know what you are thinking, "I have never said that I wanted to be perfect." Well you may not have said it in so many words, but every time you think, 'I don't want to be seen to be imperfect' that is in effect what you are saying. Our fear of failing and looking foolish will do nothing more than trap us in a world of never trying and criticizing those that do.

There has never been a prosperous person who has succeeded without at some point having to deal with being humiliated by a failure. Let me tell you about one of mine.

The fear of any performer is to have a performance before a live audience bomb. But if, perchance, that ever happens, there is a saving grace that comes with the territory; one can always fly home vowing never to return to 'that town' for a while! I, however, could not take advantage of this saving grace because the only performance I have ever blown was in my home town! My fellow townsfolk often remind me of it as they joke about how funny was my nightmare.

It happened a few years ago. A British comedian was coming to town and the organizers thought that it would be good for "our own Wes Beavis" to be the supporting artist. I was glad to help out and thought it would be a good opportunity for my fellow townsfolk to see what I do when travel to other cities and countries.

Thinking about what I could do to make the concert special, I called upon the lighting engineers to lend a hand. Knowing that the concert venue had some colored spotlights available for use, I thought it would be a good idea to hire some smoke machines to add visual effect. I had performed at many events where the use of smoke machines added to the theatrical atmosphere of a performance as splashes of color would reflect off the smoke. My technical knowledge of how these machines worked was very limited, yet the lighting engineers were happy to add their enthusiasm to mine.

The concert day arrived. It was going to be a full house. The technicians put the smoke machines in place and gave them a little test. Yes, they seemed to do what they were hired to do—blast out puffs of smoke. As I headed back stage, I could not help but feel a little apprehensive. I had performed possibly a thousand times before, but being that this performance was in my home town, I wanted this concert to go particularly well.

It was almost time for me to go on stage. My first number was going to be a 'rip it up' and get everybody excited type of song. I asked the back stage manager whether the smoke machines had started to fill the stage. He wasn't sure so using his headset intercom he asked the audio engineers situated in the main auditorium for a report. They reported that the smoke was not significantly noticeable and suggested "a few more puffs."

The smoke machines were thus thrown back into action. My request to the back stage manager was that I wanted a good level of smoke on stage. He was happy to oblige and said, "I'll just keep the machines on." There was no more time to think about it, my name was being called from main stage. It was show time!

I hit the stage with the effervescence of a thousand Alka-Seltzer tablets being tossed into a bucket of Coca-Cola. I was pumped, even if the smoke machines were not. I was about twenty seconds into my opening number when it happened. Nobody could have been pre-pared. The smoke, which was hardly noticeable when the music started playing, suddenly took over. The concert 'angel of death' made its way to the front of the stage and then moved into the audience. Like a merciless odor, it invaded every corner of the room. Then, having nowhere else to go, it started to rise. The house technicians were panicking and called to the stage manager, "No more smoke. . .No more smoke." He thought they were saying, "more smoke" so he cranked up the smoke machines to full throttle.

I watched the audience disappear into a cloud of dense fog. I knew they were still there, so I jumped off the stage into the audience hoping I could rescue the concert from the jaws of certain death. It was to no avail. Through the veil of smoke, I could see the expressions on the faces of the people. I knew it was all over. They had that 'what in blazes is this guy doing?' look of bewilderment on their faces.

I left the stage absolutely humiliated. A colleague of mine told me afterwards that the front steps to the auditorium looked like a hospital emergency ward. People were running out of the building coughing, choking, and sucking hard on their ventilen dispensers. He said it was quite a memorable sight. It took a while for the smoke to disappear, but eventually it did—along with myself. The only redeeming factor was that my performance set up the British comedian with a good cache of jokes for the rest of the evening.

Some failures you can laugh off. Some take years before you can laugh about it. On this occasion, I made the mistake of letting the failure get to me. Had I been a drinking man, I would have contemplated getting drunk to inebriate the pain. Instead, I went to the movies, hoping that a few hours in a dark room would help me to forget my failure. It didn't. Wallowing in my misery did not achieve a thing.

Looking back on this experience, I realized that most of my pain was because I did not want to be seen as being imperfect. What a trap I have learned this to be.

Do not confuse striving for excellence with wanting to be perfect. Striving for excellence is doing your best in the face of having no guarantees of success. But demanding perfection of yourself will only become fuel for a low self-opinion because the world is full of smoke

31

machines ready to steal your moment of perfection. Where does this leave you? Always feeling like you never measure up.

People who enjoy prosperity have learned, usually the hard way, that they are not perfect. They accept that there will always be times when their best is not good enough to overcome whatever the prevailing conditions. But their striving for excellence motivates them to refuse to get stuck on a failure. Instead they push through it. So whenever smoke blows your show, do what winners do: Declare it history and quickly move on!

Trap #2

My Life is a Ruined Picture

When many people view their lives, they are disappointed by what they see; the picture of their life is ruined. They consider themselves as less valuable because they carry some scars from life. It does not take too many mistakes, failures, or unfortunate experiences to make somebody feel as if they are damaged goods.

Viewing our life as a picture in the process of being painted will leave us demoralized and defeated. All it takes is a few unfortunate experiences to have the painting blighted with unwanted blemishes. Since life imposes tough experiences upon us, the picture of our life can end up being covered in unwanted splotches —looking like it has been targeted by a flock of birds.

Thus, we stand back from our life and see what could have been a beautiful picture destroyed by the imposition of things we never wanted. And from this marred picture, we draw our opinion of ourselves.

In order to release prosperity into your life, you must start to see your life not as a picture but rather as a mosaic. A mosaic is made up of thousands of little colored tiles arranged in such a way as to create a pleasing picture. When you closely examine a mosaic, rarely do the individual tiles look special. Yet, when viewed from a distance, you discover that because of their placement, every tile plays an important part in making the mosaic beautiful.

Consider your life as a mosaic. Every facet and experience of life is painted on its own little tile. So if you go through a difficult time of hardship and all you see is black, one day that black tile will find its proper place in the mosaic of your life. The wonderful thing about a mosaic is that the color of a tile that makes no sense can be made significant and even beautiful if placed the right way.

The same can be said of our experiences. Experiences that make no sense in themselves can be made significant and even beautiful if we arrange them to play a positive role in our life. If you view your life as a mosaic in the making, you never have to consider that a bad experience will declare you to be damaged goods. For whatever experience you go through, if placed in the right context, it can add richness and depth to your character.

Trap #3

If it was going to happen, it would have happened by now!

Finding oneself stalled at a certain level of achievement can easily lead to thinking, "If greater success was meant to be, it would have happened by now." This is often jumping to an inaccurate conclusion. Further success may require you to sharpen your skills or broaden your territory. But most likely it's not your lack of ability but your lack of fresh thinking which is the issue. Consider these words: If you always think what you have always thought, you'll always get what you have always got.

Our thinking is what most needs to be changed in order to advance to the next level. Jim Rohn says: "If you are not financially independent by the age of forty or fifty, it doesn't mean that you are in the wrong country. It does not mean that you live in the wrong community. Neither does it mean that you live in the wrong time nor that you're the wrong person. It simply means that you have the wrong plan."

Yes it is probably true, under your current plan, if it was going to happen, it would have happened by now. But do not resign yourself to thinking, "This is as good as I can make life to be. If I was more gifted I would have done better." Do not buckle on the shackles of this low self-opinion. It will do no more than sabotage further advancement.

With regard to your potential for success, it is never the end of the road for you. As long as you are willing to learn and grow, you can make it happen. Change your thinking, change your plan, and change your future.

Trap #4

Everybody else has their act together

Dr. Stephen Arterburn in his book *How to Win at Life Without Losing at Love* says, "If you want to win—you need to lose the wounds." Thinking that everybody else has their act together except you is an exercise in major wound licking. Your big slurping psychological tongue is lapping away at your insecurities, encouraging infective thoughts of victimization. Stop it!

So what if everybody else has their act together. At what point are we authorized to declare ourselves a victim? The answer is NEVER. As soon as you think you're a victim, of whatever circumstance, you are dead. Certainly dead to the possibility of being personally prosperous.

Believe me, I would be the first to advocate being one of the 'walking wounded' if I thought it would lead me to prosperity. What I have discovered is the opposite. Positive people stay away from you as you march your way, under the shade of the victim cloud, straight to the poorhouse.

Find out how positive people have dealt with their wounds and copy them. You are more able to act your way into a better way of feeling than to feel your way into a better way of acting. So act your way into having your act together.

Trap #5

If only I was more attractive

Okay, I am going to grant you this one. The truth is that beautiful people have to work less to be accepted. That's why they are called attractive, because others are drawn to them. There is no denying it. If you look stunningly beautiful, you will have more opportunities offered to you and an easier time gaining access to people. I recently heard Hollywood's leading cosmetic surgeon say, "Given the same skill, the one who looks the best will get the apple." So, yes, beautiful people do have an advantage. But it comes at a price—a huge price.

Most beautiful people live with the suspicion that people are attracted to them for their looks instead of their abilities and true selves. Many others do not even see themselves as beautiful. When they look in the mirror, instead of being impressed and thankful, they focus on what they perceive to be major faults. But this is not the hardest thing about being beautiful.

The hardest thing is that they never have to struggle to be noticed. "What's so tough about that?" I hear you ask. "That's a blessing not a curse," I hear you say. Wrong. It's our struggle to be noticed that drives us to define our true selves. It compels us to develop character, resolve, and abilities. It gives us the sensitivity to understand the plights of other people. Sure, being super attractive would help us in some ways. But don't think your miseries would be over. Some of the most unhappy people I have met could be models or are models already.

Character, resolve, and abilities will attract a prosperity that having a certain dress size or a full head of hair can never attract. In all your deliberations about this topic never forget this: a person who radiates confidence and joy will always be more attractive than a beautiful person who is unhappy. Thankfully, authentic beauty does not reside in something as frail as a body which cannot defy the effects of gravity and aging.

I wrote this poem a few years ago to encourage those of us who sometimes feel that we weren't in the room when the gifts of beauty were handed out.

You're So Beautiful To Me

I thought about you for ages
Even before the start of time
I contemplated everything
That went into your design

I fashioned you completely
Uniquely through and through
I didn't start with someone else
Then slightly change them into you

I thought about your future
Dreamed what you could be
Then I got to work creating
Someone the world has never seen

I thought about your appearance
And knew you'd want the looks
That would find your picture taken
And put on magazines and books

Sometimes you'll want to question
Why you look the way you do
I chose to take your beauty
And pour it all inside of you

You see, when I came to make your beauty
I decided what I'd made
Was too precious for the outside
Where the years would make it fade

So I put it all into your heart
Protected from your age
Knowing then that you could radiate
Through life at every stage

I know you still will question
And to question you are free
But be assured of this my child
You're so beautiful to me.

Wes Beavis

Ways to Build a Better Self-Opinion

Usually when we suffer bouts of low self-opinion (and we all do from time to time), we do not need professional counseling. In fact, the only counseling we need is from a loving friend who gives us the classic three word therapy: "Get over it!" But just in case you would like a little more direction than that, here are some tips that will lead to a healthier self-opinion.

1. Be less self absorbed

Self-centeredness and introspection rarely bring relief to someone struggling with a low self-opinion. The remedy for low self-opinion cannot be found within. Someone once said to me that looking inside ourselves for answers is a futile effort because we are like onions. When we work through the layers in search of our core being, we discover that we are really just the sum total of a bunch of layers.

The source of a healthy self-opinion has to come from somewhere outside of ourselves. It

41

comes from our accomplishments, the utilization of our talents, seeing our positive influence in the lives of others, and ultimately our spiritual foundations.

2. See yourself as a success

Dr. Richard Gaylord Briley in his book *Pray and Grow Rich*, says: "If you don't 'see' yourself as a success—you never will be." Sometimes, I admit, it is hard to see yourself as a success. Tough, but do it anyway. The alternative is to visualize yourself failing or giving up. If the latter be your choice, then visualize also your home in the poorhouse—it is all part of the same package.

Reinforce a self-opinion of success and victory. Dr. Denis Waitley says: "Winners dwell on and hold the self-image of that person they would most like to become."

3. Set some goals

Achieving a goal is a great way to counteract a low self-opinion. When you can point to some improvement in your life it makes you feel better. Build into your life a commitment to get to the end of each day having achieved a goal. You will discover that achieving the big goals of your life is mostly the result of your accumulated daily victories.

Remember, the major benefit of a goal is in how it motivates you to be the person you need to be in order to achieve the goal. It is who you become, more than the achievement, that is valuable. The achievement is a testimony to the expansion in the value of your life. There is a certain euphoria that comes from seeing personal growth in your life. It does wonders for how you feel about yourself. What goal can you set and achieve today?

4. Clean up your environment

If your house is a mess, clean it up! The road to prosperity is not littered with trash and junk. I have had the privilege of being invited to the homes of many outrageously prosperous people. None of them lived in a state of clutter and unattractiveness.

Some friends were once asked how they kept their house so clean. They contemplated the question and then replied, "We clean it!"

You can change an enormous amount in how you feel about yourself by cleaning up your living quarters. Your home may not be able to compete with a palace in size but it can in neatness. Shine up your self-opinion by shining up your environment.

5. Be in control of your eating and sleeping habits

I am not going to beat you over the head about being fit and healthy. We torment ourselves enough over this one. I just want to refresh your memory. Remember how good you felt about yourself when you had your eating and sleeping habits under control. Re-experience that feeling. You know you will enjoy it because you have been there before.

Again, this behavior modification costs you nothing and pays big dividends in how you feel about yourself.

6. Start saving

Regardless of how much debt you are in, start a savings account. Prove to yourself that you are taking control of your finances and spending habits. Drinking every drop from your well of wealth, leaves you feeling vulnerable and empty. Having a few bucks socked away will start to fill that empty feeling.

7. Give some money away

Again, regardless of how much debt you are in, give some money away. It does not have to be a huge amount to make a big impact on how you see yourself. There is nothing as uninspiring as spending all your money on yourself. For the modest sum of a few dollars, you can start to reverse the debilitating emptiness of being the sole recipient of your resources.

8. Drive a clean car

Instead of thinking that you need a new car, and thus putting yourself further into a prison of debt, go out and clean the car you have. I don't mean run it through the local gas station auto-wash. I mean get out there with a bucket and some rags. Put some sweat into restoring pride in the car that you currently drive.

We all know that we feel better about our vehicles when they are clean and smelling pleasant. A clean older car will always look better than an unkempt late model car anyway. Put in the effort. Not only will it restore some pride in what you already have, but you will have elevated your self-opinion without it costing you any money. When the feeling wears off, get out there and clean it again.

9. Perform an act of thoughtfulness

A few weeks ago, my wife and I took our two young boys on a road trip. We arrived in a town where we had never been before and stopped at a shopping center to pick up a few groceries. We had parked some distance from the store and in a place that was quite littered with trash. My oldest son, David, started picking up the trash and then my younger son Zachary joined in. Henceforth, being totally inspired by our kids, Eleanor and I became involved in the clean-up process.

Soon we had the whole area looking pleasant again. When the job was finished, I turned to my family and said, "See, we have only been in this town for ten minutes and already it is a better place for us being here!"

In reality, nobody would have noticed what we did or even cared. But that was not the payoff. The payoff was in how great we felt about the experience. Low self-opinion is little more than feeling a sense of worthlessness about our lives. Some task as humbling as this is often all it takes to elevate our sense of self-worth.

10. Prove your restraint

Go to a shopping mall. Do two laps of the mall on both levels and walk out having bought nothing. Prove to yourself that you have power over the powerful forces of marketing.

Restraint is like a muscle. Use it, exercise it and it will maintain its strength. Each time you exercise your restraint over destructive thoughts and actions, you are empowered. A prosperous person has strong restraint muscles.

These are just ten examples of how we can escape the shackles of a low self-opinion. The important thing is in understanding this: Just as the shackles of low self-opinion are self-imposed, they are also self-releasing. Escape from the things that enslave you and be released to savor the satisfaction of a fulfilling life—a life of prosperity.

Chapter 3

Escape from the Effects of
Your Imperfections

As he returned to the room with my x-rays, the puzzled look on my dentist's face told me something was not right. At thirteen years of age, I should have lost all my baby teeth by now. Twelve baby teeth stood as solid as ever. "Don't I have to lose these teeth before my permanent ones come through?" I asked the dentist. His response was grim. "That's the problem," he said. "Twelve permanent teeth did not form in your jaw. You still have your baby teeth because there are no permanent teeth to force them out. I'm sorry but you will never have a full set of permanent teeth." Thus, it was explained to me that due to a genetic malformation, I had been dealt a bad hand in the smile department!

That was the first time I remember the intrusion of imperfection upon my life. My two front teeth had come through but with baby teeth on either side, they accentuated the bucked tooth look. I thought, up until then, that the 'Bugs Bunny' profile was temporary. Apparently not. The dentist said that there was nothing he could do until my jaw stopped growing whereupon I could be fitted with false teeth.

Things were made worse a few months later when I was at a school track meet. I was preparing to take my final pole vaulting run. There had been a strong breeze blowing which was causing havoc on the stability of the cross bar. As pole vaulters would trot down the track ready to vault over the bar, the wind would blow the bar down. A track official decided to solve the problem by semi-affixing the bar on one of the uprights, thereby inhibiting the wind from dislodging the bar.

My final attempt was not a good one. I did not clear the bar and it cost me more than my pride. Because of the way the bar had been affixed to the upright, instead of falling straight down, it skewed sideways and I fell on it face first. It snapped one of my 'Bugs Bunny' teeth clean off near the gumline. Needless to say, I had an interesting smile for the next few years—one big permanent tooth hanging down like a monumental stalactite. The dentist eventually put a plastic crown over what remained of the broken tooth but this didn't help much. The real battle was no longer an external issue, but an internal one.

Every one of us bears some imperfection. While some imperfections are more obvious than others, each of us have things about ourselves we would change in a heartbeat if we could. You can reason all day with someone as to whether their perceived imperfection is worth their concern. In the end, you will never change their mind if they believe they are debilitated in some way.

The tragedy is that most people allow their imperfections to manifest far deeper consequences than necessary. Og Mandino says: "Never fret at any imperfections that you fear may impede your progress. While life may not always be fair, you must never allow the pains, hurdles, and handicaps of the moment to poison your attitude and plans for yourself and your future. You can never win when you are wearing the ugly coat of self-pity, and the sour sound of whining will certainly frighten away any opportunity for success."

How to Escape the Effects of Our Imperfections

The greatest power of an imperfection is what happens internally as we ponder upon the imperfection. Whatever mountain that we face on the outside is nothing compared to the mountain of intimidation that it can create inside. The internal struggle is everything. The longer you dwell on your misfortunes the greater their power to harm you. Here are some ways to win the internal struggle:

Take advantage of external remedies

Sometimes there will be external remedies for our imperfections. By all means avail yourself of the benefits of scientific developments and achievements. Recently, I watched a program about two reconstructive surgeons who travel to Third World countries to help children who are burdened with severe physical deformities. The program followed one child's progress from being pitifully debilitated to being given a new life thanks to the skill of these two doctors. What they did was miraculous.

If there is a safe external remedy to your situation, use it to your advantage. A lot of confidence can be gained by corrective and cosmetic therapies. I now have fourteen false teeth that give me a great smile thanks to the advances of modern dentistry. Being the beneficiary of scientific advances, I am a believer that in some situations this is the right answer.

Of course, this is often the easiest solution. That is why there will always be a vast trail of people exploring this solution first. Unfortunately, while it can be an answer in many cases, some who try this solution come away dissatisfied. Some challenges have to be fought and won on the internal battlefield.

Don't incubate your inadequacies

My sister-in-law Sue has been a great source of inspiration to me. She is an attractive and lovely woman yet she has lived her whole life with the challenge of being born with no fingers on her left hand.

One day, I mustered the courage to ask Sue whether she ever had days where the condition of her hand 'got her down'. She responded, "Wes, I can't afford to. I can't afford to let it get me down because there is nothing I can do to change it." Sue had made up her mind at a certain point in her life to accept that which she could not change and to make the most of what she had left. Consequently, she is a beautiful woman who never notices her hand so neither do other people.

Miracle solutions are great and we should use them if they're available. But where there is no miracle solution, we must refuse to pamper the imperfection.

One time, upon hearing about a basketball team needing a player, I phoned the coach and offered my services. His first question was: "Are you over six foot?" When I said no, he simply hung up on me. There was nothing I could do to change the fact that I was not over six feet tall.

Our lives are full of times where we are faced with the reality of our inadequacies. What are we to do? Here is the number one rule: Never incubate your inadequacies. Never nurture your shortcomings. Never coddle your failures. Don't dwell on your misfortunes. If you do, it's straight to the poorhouse for you—the club-house of pity parties.

Going through the ordeal with my teeth, I thought my parents were heartless, uncaring and incapable of compassion. They seemed to carry on with life as though my trauma was not a big deal. They never gave me the go ahead to consider myself a victim. Darn them, I thought, they're not even commiserating with me. What type of parents are they?

In retrospect, in such a situation, they were the best parents to have. The last thing I needed was a 'green light' to feel sorry for myself. Not that I didn't feel sorry for myself—I did! I became quite adept at throwing pity parties. The only problem was that I was the only one to show up to the party. I did not like the person I was becoming. Sure enough, I figured it was not the absence of teeth but the presence of a bad attitude that made me ugly.

Be gracious to yourself about your imper-fections. In reality, no one else cares. Wake up to the fact that nurturing your shortcoming is what disadvantages you, not the shortcoming itself. Get the picture? Don't fill your dents with laments. Nothing highlights a dent more than filling it with your laments. Perfection has never been a prerequisite for prosperity.

Don't look for peace in someone else's head

Bayless Connelly, one of my favorite speakers, recently said something which made profound sense to me: "You'll never find peace in somebody else's head. You will never fulfill your destiny as long as you are tyrannized by what other people think of you." Our desire to be accepted by others conditions us to look for peace in somebody else's head. We think, "If only I could be accepted by an individual (or crowd), then it would be easy to accept myself."

So, to this end, we do things to compensate for our imperfections: purchase a stylish car, get cosmetic surgery, diet compulsively, or have an affair. All the while we think that by engaging in such activities, we will gain the approval of other people and thus be more able to accept ourselves. Trying to find peace in somebody else's head never works.

Peace is best found amidst your imperfections by first accepting them. Then, forget them, and get on with developing your strengths.

Identify your vulnerable times

Even though you may have slain the dragon of your imperfections, sometimes you will still feel his breath. Generally, the combination of being physically tired and the length of time since your last victory can lead you to revisiting your imperfections.

Resist becoming a casualty of your vulnerable moments. Dr. David Smith, a leading clinical psychologist, gives this advice: "Identify your vulnerable times and endeavor to have tasks in which to keep yourself busy. You must do this, otherwise you will entertain discouraging thoughts and set yourself on a course to annihilating any sense of self-worth."

Everybody goes through times of feeling 'blue' about their imperfections. The first step is to not harass yourself. It is okay to have fallen short. It only becomes a problem if it stops you from moving forward. The second step is to realize that entertaining regret accomplishes nothing more than sending you lower. The further you allow yourself to slide away on the downward spiral, the harder it is to come back. In the end, regret is a big waste of energy.

One of the best things to know about experiencing low times is that they do pass. As surely as they come, they do go away. It's just a matter of time. As long as you do not make negative destiny decisions in your low times, you will ride them out and emerge the winner for having done so. I wrote a poem, *It Will Pass*, to help me focus positively during such times. Take a copy of it and put it somewhere obvious so that you can refer to it the next time you go through a tough period.

It Will Pass

When it comes to the moment when you're tempted to ask,
Why are things never easy, why always a task?
Why does it take longer and always cost more?
Why does disappointment find a way to my door?

The answer is simple and this you must learn,
The world owes you nothing what you gain you must earn,
It doesn't come easy to those who achieve,
They all have their setbacks and reasons to grieve.

There will always be days when plans come unstuck,
It might be your fault if it's not from bad luck,
When something has failed, you can't change the fact,
The only change you can make is in how you react.

Anyone can be happy when the going is kind,
It's when things fall apart that a champion's defined,
A champion sets time to work through the sorrow
But once time is up they move on to tomorrow

They avoid the temptation to go down the track,
Of despairing so much that it's hard to come back,
They know that success is assured if they last,
And whatever the grief, they know it will pass.

Wes Beavis

Let them make you, not break you

Studies have proven the strong link between being disadvantaged and having a determination to succeed. It really is quite simple. People have the choice to let their imperfections be the breaking of them or the making of them. Great people develop tremendous strengths often as a response to compensating for their weaknesses. Instead of focusing on what is wrong with you, focus on what things are right with you.

Take a piece of paper and at the top write: Things I am good at doing. Then make your list. Having made your list, write out your life's mission statement based on your list. Then work your life according to your mission statement. People who are working according to their mission in life have fewer pity parties. They do not need them because they are allowing their positive traits to determine their state of mind rather than their negative traits.

I love the story of a tourist who arrived in a small and quaint town in Europe. He sat down on a park bench next to an elderly man and asked the elderly man this question: "Were there any great men born in this town?" The elderly man sat quietly for a few moments then replied, "No. . . just babies."

Great people are grown, not born. Don't drag your dreams down to the level of your imperfections but rather, push your imperfections in the direction of your dreams.

Chapter 4

Escape from the Influence of
Depreciating People

Eleanor and I purchased a home knowing it would be a temporary accommodation. Like many other people, we had desires for a dream home. We knew that the dream home would come in due time as our business became more and more established. Until then, we drew upon the virtue of patience.

But one day, my patience ran out. We had just been through a period of having two families stay with us. We had more people per square foot of house than what I felt was comfortable for our guests. I had a choice. Scale back on our offers of hospitality or get a bigger house. I didn't want to do the former and I was not in a position to do the latter. So what did I do? I jumped in the car and went looking for our dream house!

For two hours, I drove around the city in search of our next home. I drove into one street that was double sized in width and ended with a huge cul-de-sac. My mind pictured teaching my boys to rollerblade in the safety of that cul-de-sac. Every house on the street was wonderful and I was particularly drawn to the two homes at the end of the street.

Characteristically, when developers divide up the land in a cul-de-sac they apportion it to be occupied by three or four houses, giving each house in the cul-de-sac a small front yard that widens out to a larger backyard. In this situation though, they decided not to do that. The huge cul-de-sac was shared only by two homes, giving each home extensive open parkland. I thought that either home would be incredible to own. The elevation of the house on the left gave it a terrific outlook upon the city lights. "That would be my first pick," I thought as I drove away. There were only two challenges. I didn't have the funds and not one house on the street was for sale. Ah, one can still dream!

Some time later, I was hosting a community

dinner for two hundred and forty business people. As I was contemplating the special guest list, I decided to invite Chuck, the managing director of a construction company, and his wife Jackie. Chuck's construction team had recently finished the beautiful buildings that would house the banquet. I was enamored by the positive charm of this couple and was delighted for the opportunity to build the relationship.

In the course of dinner conversation with Chuck and Jackie, I learned that they lived in the same neighborhood where I had seen the 'dream home'. I told Jackie that I loved that area and I wanted to live there one day. Jokingly, I remarked, "If a house near you comes on the market, call me." Aware that patter like this is often forgotten, I thought nothing more about it.

Three months later I received a phone call from Jackie: "Wes, a house in our area has just come on the market. Are you still interested?" She gave me the street name and house number but no other information. Driving into the neighborhood, I looked for the house that matched the address Jackie had given me. I couldn't believe my eyes. It was the house on the left side of the cul-de-sac. The very house that months before I had chosen.

In the months since first seeing the home, our business had flourished to the point that we had enough to put down a thirty percent cash deposit. We bought the home that night. A dream and a dinner invitation to the right person can go a long way!

The point I want to make in relating this story is this: More of your dreams will come true if you keep company with the right people.

Depreciating People

In the first mile of owning a new car, the value of the car drops by twenty-five percent. Over the following years, the car continues to depreciate in value. When you stop to think about it, people can have this same depreciating quality. The value of their life diminishes over time. This is how it happens.

For some reason, the gravitational pull of life is towards negativity. If we don't make a conscious decision to override this natural inclination then we naturally become negative. We'll find ourselves being more at home with fear than faith, more comfortable with doubt than belief and more able to criticize than praise. The problem with these negative traits is that they cannot grow positive results.

If we submit to the gravitational pull of negative thoughts and actions, the end result is that we find our value diminishing because of the way we think and live our lives. Having a negative disposition means we are gradually losing the ability to add value to life and with each passing day, we lose ground.

There are two battles we must fight in order to become prosperous. The first battle is to confront our own depreciating tendencies and overcome them. The second battle is to overcome the influence of depreciating people around us.

You can easily tell when you are under the influence of a depreciating person. You leave their presence feeling empty, pessimistic and thinking less about yourself. On the other hand, when you leave the presence of an appreciating person you feel more valuable and positive. You sense that the appreciating person has added value to your life.

If you want prosperity in your life, you must escape from the influence of depreciating people. In some instances, such as the case of a depreciating spouse or family member, you may not be able to escape their presence. But you can always escape their influence. Here are five ways in which you can:

1. Release them

Many people have power in our lives only because we have appointed them to that position of influence. Each one of us has the right to choose our own advisors.

If there is someone in your life who makes you miserable, it is because you have given them the right to influence you this way. Regardless of what they are doing to make you irritable, your response is still your choice. "But he makes me so mad!" you say. That is not true. He just provides the right conditions. You decide to be mad in response to those conditions. The more we react, the more we reinforce their power in our lives.

It is rarely easy but unless we escape their influence, we will never rise above them. Consider what Dr. David Schwartz said: "Release them or you will start to resemble them." Simply retire the depreciating person from your board of directors and install an appreciating person in their place.

2. Recognize their area of expertise

I had breakfast with a businessman recently who relayed to me this experience. He had offered a business opportunity to a man named Simon who expressed enthusiastic interest. Having covered all the details, they made an appointment to meet again at a later date, thus giving Simon the opportunity to share the idea with his wife.

When they got together again, it was obvious to my friend that Simon had completely cooled on the business venture. Assuming that Simon's wife was not in agreement, my friend asked what it was about the proposal his wife didn't like. Simon said, "Oh, it's not my wife. She is okay with the idea but I talked it over with my dad. He said that it was a waste of time and told me that I should not get involved."

My friend was astute and asked, "Simon, tell me, what does your father do for a living?" Simon's reply was that his dad was a mechanic. He then asked, "Simon, is it possible that your dad's expertise does not extend to understanding this business?" Simon concurred that while his dad was an excellent automotive engineer, he did not have any level of expertise in relation to the business venture that Simon was considering.

Many people will accept the depreciating advice from their family members out of respect for them even though they may not have any level of expertise upon which to base their judgments. We can easily miss out on great opportunities because we gain our counsel from all the wrong people. Evaluate the person's expertise to be commenting on a particular issue. They might be well intentioned in their counsel but not experienced enough for their counsel to be wise.

The next time you are tempted to take the advice of a nay-sayer, look at their lives and ask yourself if you want to become like them. By taking their advice, you set yourself on the road to becoming like them.

Postscript: Simon joined the business and has become so successful that he will be able to retire before his father.

3. Realize that you cannot bat someone else's ball game

The sad reality is that not all depreciating people want to be helped. Submission to the gravitational pull of negativity is easier than fighting to override it. Improving life requires work which some could not be bothered doing.

It is perplexing to watch someone gifted and full of potential let their lives go to waste. Yet there is nothing we can do to help them unless they are willing to change their behavior and thinking. You cannot force positive change upon people. If that were possible, our prison rehabilitation programs would work.

Many people become stalled on their journey to prosperity because they are trying to become everybody's savior. To reach out and help someone is noble. To help someone more than they want to be helped is foolish. There is a saying: "Don't try and teach a hog to sing, it will frustrate you and annoy the heck out of the hog."

Stop batting other people's ball games for them. It achieves little in the short term and does nothing for the long run.

Release yourself from the notion that you are everybody's savior. You are not being cold hearted by abandoning misguided nobility. Even the greatest physician of them all first asked the question, "Do you want to be well?"

If a person really wants to move forward, by all means, help them back on to their feet. This is the right thing to do. The wrong thing to do, however, is to solve other people's problems for them. All this will do is cause you to despair over the results and lead you to becoming cynical about people.

4. Do not live for the approval of others

This sounds wrong doesn't it? You may be thinking, "If I do not have the approval of my boss, I will lose my job," or, "If I don't seek the approval of my friends, I will lose them," or, "If I don't seek the approval of my landlord, I might lose my home." Wrong, wrong, wrong!

If you base your life on gaining the approval of others, what happens? You become like a poll-driven politician, whose decisions are determined by what would gain the approval of the most people. You become someone who twists and turns in order to gain people's favor. It is a way of life that does work, to a certain degree, but it is an awful and insecure life to live. You are always trying to read people's minds and change yourself to suit their ever changing whims.

Don't act a certain way in order to be liked. This is simply being manipulating. Instead, *act according to your principles*; for example, I will always do my best to be productive in the tasks given to me, and to be an encouragement to my fellow man. If this is a principle that you live by, then you need not anguish over whether your boss likes you. And if your boss moves on, living by this principle means you need not worry about appealing to the favor of the new boss in order to keep your job. Personalities will always change, but sound principles do not.

Be principle driven in the way you live your life. Choose friends based on your principles. Work according to your principles. Make business transactions according to your principles. You will find the going a lot easier and prosperity will more readily flow to you. When you live by the right principles, you will have the approval of the right people. It will be inevitable.

5. Seek the company of appreciating people

The more time you spend associating with appreciating people, the less time you will be spending under the influence of people who are losing value. This, in itself, is enough to bring about radical change. Yet, there is more. Spending time with appreciating people causes you to absorb their values and view of life.

If you put a group of people in a room who do not know each other, given enough time, each will gravitate to others like themselves. It is amazing to watch how non-producers will naturally gravitate to the company of other non-producers, how critics will find other critics, and how dreamers will be attracted to other dreamers. If you want a life of prosperity, you must seek out dynamic people and do all you can to be in their company.

When I was playing basketball seriously, I discovered an interesting principle at work. Occasionally, I would have the opportunity to play with a team outside of my grade level if they were a player short. When there was an opening with a team in a lower grade, I would see it as an opportunity to have my superior abilities shine. Yet, it hardly ever worked that way. I would inevitably play scrappy and would often foul out of the game. It seemed that sinking to the level of the other players was easier than lifting them up to my level of ability.

Inversely, whenever I joined a team of a higher grade, I would surprise myself by keeping up with them. The better players brought out the better player in me. This helped me to realize that our environment can make all the difference in how we perform.

You can have major influence over your performance by simply being more astute in choosing your environment. Take the initiative in building relationships with the right people. Choose to be with people who bring out your best performance. Prosperity comes more readily to those who do!

Chapter 5

Escape from the Thinking that
Keeps You Broke

In many countries of the world people work like slaves just to maintain impoverishment. Thankfully, here in the land of opportunity, this does not happen. Or does it? Think about this a little longer and you will realize that this is exactly what many of us do. We work relentlessly just to maintain a state of being broke. How could this be? We live in a rich land, fertile with good things and the opportunity to enjoy them. In such an environment, how could we find ourselves in a state of being broke? Easily. We think our way into a state of impoverishment.

A year ago, a friend named Foley was visiting from abroad and he was passing through Los Angeles. While staying at our place, he looked at a map of the greater Los Angeles area and realized Mexico was only a few hours south of our home. He asked whether there would be any chance of paying a quick visit to Mexico since he was so close. It sounded like a great idea and I suggested that we visit Tijuana, a city just inside the Mexican border.

Prior to leaving, I insisted that Foley check to be sure he had his passport in his possession. In fact, I asked him several times. I knew that it is very easy to get into Mexico but impossible to return to the United States without proper travel documents. My wife, Eleanor, concerned about my welfare, asked whether I had my passport. "No worries," was my quick retort, "I have a California driver's license which proves my residency in the United States. . . that's all I need!" Foley and I then left in pursuit of our excellent Mexican adventure.

True to expectation, crossing the border into Mexico was as easy as walking through the turnstiles of K-Mart. Nobody was there to question our entry. Foley and I walked right into Mexico without another thought and spent the next few hours there. It was almost midnight when we decided to head home.

Arriving at the U.S. border, we found our way through to customs and proceeded to gain entry back into the United States. Foley went first, showed his travel documents and was promptly signalled through. I took out my California driver's license and showed it to the customs official. She was in the process of waving me through when I thought to strike up a conversation with her while I put my license back into my wallet. The customs room was largely deserted except for Foley and me. I thought that she would appreciate a little late night chit-chat. Bad move Wes. Picking up on my foreign accent, she proceeded to ask me whether I was a citizen of the United States.

I told her that I was a permanent resident of the United States. She re-asked the question: "Are you a citizen of the United States?" I knew that I had not lived in the U.S. long enough to qualify for citizenship so I had to tell her the truth, "No, I am not a citizen, but I want to be!" She did not see the humor in my response. She quickly motioned for a guard to come and detain me. The guard led me to an interrogation room for questioning leaving Foley totally bewildered.

For over an hour, I was questioned about my attempt to enter the United States illegally. I told them that I was under the impression that since I was a U.S. resident and held a State of California driver's license, the need for me to bring my passport was negated. They informed me that my impression was seriously wrong.

In the end, I was given a choice on how to remedy the situation. I could go back into Mexico, phone Eleanor, and ask her to bring my passport to me. I looked at my watch. It was almost 1:00 AM. I thought about what I would say to her, "Honey, I know it's late but can you bring my passport to Mexico?" I was pretty sure her love for me would have extended to waking the children, loading them into the car, and driving for two hours to the border. But I did not think this was the right time to test such love.

I considered option two. It was much better. The customs agents were able to ascertain from computer records that I was indeed a current legal resident of the United States. All I needed to do then was to pay a one hundred dollar fine and fill in a few documents to be re-admitted to the United States. Letting my wife continue in her peaceful slumber, I paid my one hundred dollars and headed for home.

This experience taught me that no amount of confidence can turn a wrong assumption into right assumption. Clearly, I had allowed my thoughts to lead me into a bad situation.

When you examine the troubles that people get themselves into, it is often because they confidently conclude their wrong assumptions are right. Here are some assumptions that keep people broke:

Assumption #1

Image is everything

If you were to look at the advertising in any women's magazine, you would be surely convinced that image is the key to life. Instead of stating, "This perfume smells really good and your man will like it," the full page simply has the picture of a stunning model in an idyllic setting. The name of the perfume is placed insignificantly on the page as if it didn't really matter.

In reality, the name of the perfume does not matter because the advertisers aren't trying to sell the perfume inasmuch as they are selling the image. The advertisers know that if the image is bought, the perfume will sell with little consideration for the price. People willingly make the purchases thinking that by buying the product, they will be transformed into the exquisite life that the model is representing.

Wanting a successful image is a huge trap for people. They want success so they buy the things that make them look successful in the hope that one day their success will arrive. Then, their success will enable them to pay for the image they have already purchased. In reality, that day never comes because their debts stop them from ever experiencing the prosperity needed to be successful.

The only people who should buy such items are the ones who can pay cash for them. Interestingly enough, studies of genuinely wealthy people have shown that they do not buy items for the sake of portraying a successful image. On the whole, they see no need to spend their earnings in the pursuit of gaining an image. Their confidence is based in other things.

In some areas of life, it's important to 'fake it until you make it'. But when it comes down to faking it on credit, you have only made 'making it' that much harder.

We all want to be held in high esteem by others. This is basic to our nature. There is nothing wrong with wearing nice clothes, driving fine automobiles, and living in beautiful homes, unless you are crippling yourself in the process of acquiring them. Present an image of yourself that is true to your level of achievement.

Spending *beyond your means* for the sake of an image adds enormous pressure to your life. In the end, it makes it harder for you to attain the prosperity that you are meant to have.

Some time ago, I set the goal that our family should be debt free. When we finally paid off our home and cleared the debts on our vehicles and investments, it felt so good that we decided to never get into debt again. Consequently, we have one nice vehicle which my wife uses to transport our kids. But to date, due to our commitment to being debt free, my car is modest. Perhaps it is too modest for some situations.

Recently I met with a business colleague in Beverly Hills. In the midst of our meeting, he told me that my car was not congruent with my message of successful living. He was right. I have been blessed with a level of success that would enable me to drive a luxury foreign import. Sometimes, I wrestle with the temptation to buy one.

My challenge is that I do not want to buy a vehicle unless I can pay for it without going into debt. Then, when I do save the money required to purchase a new vehicle, I balk at the opportunity to buy. The depreciation of value that besets a car once it is driven off the showroom floor deters me. What appeals to me more is to invest the savings in a fund that doubles in value. This does more to bring the sense of freedom to my life than any nice convertible ever will.

The time will come when I will drive the car of my dreams, but not right now. Currently, more fulfillment is being derived from living debt free than having an image for which I am making re-payments.

A rule of prosperity is to not buy something for image sake until you have saved the dollars to pay for it in cash. By then, you will discover that saving the amount of money will make you feel more prosperous than any image item purchased on credit.

Assumption #2

Shopping makes me feel better

Yes it does! The experts call this 'consumption therapy.' It is a nice thing to do when we're feeling a little 'blue'—visit our favorite mall and buy a few things. What we purchase is rarely what we need but we are easily able to convince ourselves otherwise. More often than not, the purchases are made with the help of a credit card because we don't actually have the cash to pay for it.

Knowing the public's weakness for instant gratification and a good deal, many stores offer an additional ten percent savings if the customer opens a credit card account. With a phone call and social security number, the world of credit is made available. And to the uninformed, it seems an offer too good to pass. What the credit card company knows is that it will get its ten percent back many times over. Studies have conclusively proven that people buy more when they use a card rather than cash.

The problem with shopping as self-therapy is that it is a major contributor to why we were feeling 'blue' in the first place. People spend when they feel trapped by a hectic or dull life. And being in debt is the major cause of a hectic or dull life. Thinking that shopping will make you feel better will keep you broke. It perpetuates an existence where you are constantly needing to feed the need to feel better.

One of the discoveries you will make when you become debt free is that your drive to spend money will significantly diminish. With a decreased need to spend you find the process of saving requires far less effort. Prosperity naturally comes to you when you escape the lifestyle of spending in order to feel better.

Assumption #3

I have to be better than the Jones's

We live in a society where, with the help of easy credit, we can look as good as anyone else. Never borrow money to look good. Why? Because while your flash purchases may look good, you will always look and feel like a harried hamster running on the treadmill of life just to pay for what you have bought to look good.

There's nothing that speaks of success more than the peaceful, easy confidence that one exhibits when they are living debt free. Leave the Jones's alone. Be inspired by them if you have to, but remember keeping up with the Jones's may also mean keeping up with their high level of debt.

Assumption #4

They don't like me

We all love to be liked. So it is only natural to want people to respond positively to us. The challenge arises, however, when people do not respond to us the way we want. Our reaction is to make assumptions as to why. Often those assumptions are wrong. The classic wrong assumption when people don't respond the way we want is, "They must not like me." Such thinking will keep you broke both relationally and financially.

Dr. Richard Carlson calls this thinking,

"imputing malignant motives into the actions of others." Sounds clinical, doesn't it? It simply means reading into the responses of others the thought that they don't like you. Thinking like this will lead you straight down the path to impoverishment. When your mind constantly defaults to negative assumptions such as, "They didn't return my phone call, they must not like me," or, "They didn't buy what I was selling, I must be a terrible sales person," you are programming a negative self-belief into your mind. It will cause you to suffer relationally and will also reduce your ability to succeed financially.

Let me tell you about a time when I committed this error of imputing malignant motives into someone's response. Ann Tyler was the leader of an organization that contacted me about performing at four events. It was a great opportunity.

Arriving at the first event, I looked for Ann but she was nowhere to be found. Finally she arrived just moments before the event began. We could only talk briefly because the meeting was about to get underway.

My performance made me feel great and I was confident that Ann would have been very happy. Yet she seemed detached when I spoke to her. Quickly packing up, I concluded on my journey home that my delivery must have fallen short of her expectations.

A few days later, my conclusions had so fermented that I decided to call Ann and give her the opportunity to find someone else for the remaining events. When she answered the phone, her opening line was, "Wes, I must apologize for the other day." "Apologize?" I thought. She went on to say: "You left in such a hurry that I thought I must have offended you."

I explained that my quick departure was based on my thinking that she was uninspired by my efforts. Ann then went on to clarify the situation. She explained that her sister had given birth to a baby that morning. Because she had stayed up all night with her sister, Ann had been preoccupied with getting through the morning meeting without collapsing. Wow, did I ever jump to the wrong conclusion. She wasn't detached, she was exhausted!

I had committed the cardinal sin of imputing malignant motives into her actions. I was thinking, "She doesn't like me," when that was not the issue at all. Thankfully, the occasion was redeemed and I went on to complete the remaining events.

Many people give up on potential relationships, potential sales, and potential business opportunities because they make an incorrect assumption about what the other person is thinking. If in doubt about their response, do not default to thinking the worst. Rather, think the best. Pursue the potential until the *facts*, not your impressions, tell you to move on.

Assumption #5

I have a secure job with good benefits

Is there such thing as a secure job? Since your employer has the capacity to change your hours, lay you off due to a 'downturn in the economy', or worse, fire you, there is no secure job. Even if you feel that your job is above these possibilities, corporate mergers have an amazing way of making indispensable people redundant.

A boss will only love you as long as you are needed. When you are no longer needed, there is no sentiment that will stop you from being the recipient of the 'sorry, we're going to have to let you go' speech.

Whether or not there is such a thing as a secure job with good benefits is beside the point. The question we should be asking our-selves is: "Who should be the one to determine how much I am worth?" Too many people have let their bosses determine their value. Most people are worth more than the wage they are paid. That's why I am an advocate of having your own business. When you involve yourself in enterprise *you* become the one who determines how much you are worth. You determine the limit to your income.

Doctors Stanley and Danko compiled a twenty year study of how people become wealthy in the book, *The Millionaire Next Door.* Based on their findings, they determined that self-employed people make up less than twenty percent of the workers in America but account for two-thirds of the millionaires.

While there are unique challenges involved in being your own boss, it is a far better avenue for exploring your potential for prosperity. Being involved in some form of enterprise releases your entrepreneurial spirit. Until you give this spirit flight, you will never know the heights of which you are capable.

A secure job with good benefits may give you a reasonable altitude. However, why settle for a 'reasonable' altitude, if, by releasing your entrepreneurial spirit, you are able to reach the altitude of your dreams.

Now don't call your boss and put in your resignation just yet. The last thing you want is to put a halt to your current income stream so that you can start a business. This would do little more than throw you further into debt. The best business opportunities can be established part-time. Once the business has developed to the point of sustaining your budget, then you can resign from your job and go full throttle in the pursuit of prosperity.

Thinking that you have a secure job with great benefits could be the very thinking that keeps you from experiencing prosperity.

Assumption #6

I want it while I'm young enough to enjoy it

This is the assumption that credit card companies use in encouraging young people into a life of debt. Recently, my wife and I attended a meeting of four hundred high school students. The students were asked how many had received applications for credit cards. We watched the hands of more than half the students go up. Never before have young people been so encouraged to have it all, right now.

Thinking 'I want it while I'm young enough to enjoy it' will make you old. Constantly spending everything you earn and then going into debt because you lack patience ages you. You end up working twice as much to cover the never ending re-payments.

On the other hand, having a goal and working towards it will keep you young. Delayed gratification actually extends your life. You carry less anxieties about owing money and you haven't seduced yourself into thinking that the best of life has to be enjoyed before you turn thirty-five.

Assumption #7

I can't live without it

Yeah, sure! Please allow me to say a few remarks at your funeral. "Here lies Jimmy. He died because he never got what he just *had* to have. May he rest in peace!"

Seriously, if you find yourself under severe pressure to buy something ask yourself: "How have I survived up to now without it?" Then, sleep on it for a week. Many times, you will discover the urge has passed.

Assumption #8

I got off to a bad start

Do not let your bad start in life become your excuse for passing up on a life of prosperity. Studies have conclusively shown that the greatest percentage of successful people had a rocky beginning to life. Those who conducted these studies also discovered that the rough beginning was the very thing that gave them determination. It made them determined to work towards a great finish.

Be thankful for your bad start. There's only one direction to go and that is up! Having a bad start is the best start to have. It makes a life of prosperity all the sweeter.

Assumption #9

I can afford the payments

Yes, you may be able to afford the payments, but can you afford what the payments will do to you?

Our stress levels go up in direct proportion to how many people have rights to our money. "Can I afford the payments?" is the wrong question to be asking yourself. The more appropriate question is: "Do I want another person in my life garnishing my freedom?"

Assumption #10

It's a great tax deduction

This is usually what you say when you are trying to convince yourself that buying the desired item is a sensible thing to do. People who think like this believe that a tax deduction means you get to keep more money in your pocket. The opposite is true. The reality is that, in most cases, you have to blow a dollar in interest to save yourself forty cents in tax (less if you're not in the top tax bracket). At the end of the day, you are still a dollar less prosperous. The only true 'great tax deduction' will be explored in chapter eight.

Assumption #11

I'm not good at saving money

Who is good at saving? Saving is hard. It is an acquired ability. Spending is much easier. Unless you have lived through a depression, you are more likely to be environmentally educated to spend rather than save.

Admit to the fact that saving is a learned behavior and start developing that quality within you. When you can say to yourself, "I am good at saving," you are destined to be living in prosperity.

Assumption #12

I want my kids to have the things I never had

The best things that you can give your children are your time, your good example and positive opportunities. The worst things you can give them are money and possessions. Often, wealthy parents, in their quest to give their children the life they never had, actually end up robbing their children of that very thing which made them so successful—the need to make something of their lives.

Studies have shown that few children of wealthy parents ever exhibit the personal productivity or drive of their parents. What's worse, by subsidizing your children's or your grandchildren's lives you have set yourself up to have your children always being in a state of economic dependence upon you.

Assumption #13

I can't afford to give

This is what we say when our expenses have sucked the last drop from our well of wealth. It is only logical to recognize that you cannot give what you do not have to give.

A friend of mine shared with me the story of Shotgun Charlie. Whenever my friend would go on a long car journey, Charlie would come along to keep him company. He was just like the shotgun toting companion to a stagecoach driver of old times. Hence, Charlie was given the name Shotgun.

Before Shotgun Charlie retired, he owned a barber shop in Los Angeles. He would often have famous people come in for a hair cut. For twenty years, Charlie would regularly cut the hair of billionaire Howard Hughes. Although all of Shotgun Charlie's clients tipped him, which was the customary thing to do, not once did he ever receive a tip from Howard Hughes.

Giving has nothing to do with the availability of spare money. You give because it is the right thing to do. It's impossible to experience prosperity if you don't give. In fact, giving is the supreme indicator of prosperity.

Continue to think that you can't afford to give if you want to. That's okay. Prosperity is patient. It can wait your whole life if need be. Is this what you really want? No. Then don't delay the coming of prosperity to you any longer. Rearrange your lifestyle so that you can start giving. It may only start as a small amount but its effect will be huge. By doing so, you will begin to experience feelings of prosperity.

So many sacrifice their future prosperity by holding these false assumptions. Remember, no amount of conviction can make a wrong assumption right. Becoming a millionaire in the quality of life depends on you following the escape route. Avoid the thinking that keeps you broke.

Chapter 6

Escape from the Habits that
Put You in Slavery

"The only difference between those who have failed and those who have succeeded lies in the difference of their habits. Good habits are the key to success. Bad habits are the unlocked doors to failure." Og Mandino

Mr. Durham was an uncharacteristic fifth grade teacher. As a World War II veteran, he had a ruggedness about his demeanor and teaching style. I always remember seeing him with a great wad of chewing tobacco stuffed between his lower teeth and lip. One day, a group of fellow fifth graders gathered around his desk as he relayed stories about being a soldier in World War II. I took the opportunity to ask him why he chewed tobacco. Mr. Durham's reason was simple. Lighting a cigarette in a fox hole at night was not a smart move if you wanted to see the light of the next day. He said that when the war ended he kept on chewing. So every few minutes while he taught Social Studies, Mr. Durham would slip outside and spit before resuming the lesson.

Had they known about Attention Deficit Disorder back in the early seventies, I am sure such a condition would have explained my behavior. I had an inability to sit still in class. Or maybe, I just loved socializing. Either way, there were many occasions when Mr. Durham felt it necessary to deal with my behavior. If there was a rowdy outbreak in the classroom, you could be assured to find me a major cause of the chaos.

Now having a wad of foreign matter cradled in your bottom lip does change the way you enunciate. So when Mr. Durham called my name it was unmistakable that he was the one seeking my attention. He had a low southern drawl which was made unique by the way he would carefully project his words, so as to not spill any tobacco juice. "Whereshle-e-ey. . ." he would drawl, "I'm s-s-sick an' tired of yer behavior. Step out in the hall!"

A hush would immediately come over the classroom as I headed out into the hallway that ran the entire length of the school. Mr. Durham, retrieving his finely crafted birch paddle from its place of storage, would follow behind. School policy was for a teacher to have the presence of another teacher to witness the administration of punishment. Once the witnessing teacher was in place, Mr. Durham would ask me to bend over and touch my toes. Raising the birch paddle high above his head, he would swing the paddle down on a trajectory that would intersect with my butt.

The first swat was more startling than painful. It was the moment when the nerve endings in the butt cheeks cleared the lines of communication with the pain receptors in the brain. That's why the second swat was always the hardest. The nerve endings in the butt were now sending clear and painful signals to the brain. In response to the second swat, the brain would put out an emergency call for all spare blood to immediately report to the butt cheeks to help cool the heat. It was a major lesson in the law of physics. Energy from an object in motion will always transfer its energy into the object which stops that motion. Thus, the motion energy of the flying paddle became heat energy in my butt cheeks. Needless to say, I never liked physics.

After the third swat, Mr. Durham would stand me up, look me in the eyes and say: "Whereshle-e-ey, I do believe I am looking at a changed man!" Sure enough, that was true. I would walk back into the classroom with a changed attitude and behavior.

Growing up, I had many people like Mr. Durham in my life. Their efforts to keep me on the right track were a great benefit. Yet their disciplinary guidance stopped, as it does for all of us, upon reaching adulthood.

The coming of age transfers the responsibility for our behavior to no one other than ourselves. Unless you are breaking the law, no one is going to stop you from engaging in destructive inclinations. You might have someone call your actions into question but even this is rare. Usually, if you become destructive and negative in your behavior, people will let you continue down that path. As long as your depreciating traits are not affecting the quality of their lives, they will step aside to let you march right down to the poorhouse. No Mr. Durhams will be saying, "Step out in the hall. . . let's modify your behavior."

The responsibility to keep our thinking and actions on track is entirely ours. Unfortunately, too many people do not succeed. As a result, they end up enslaved to habits that keep them from ever seeing prosperity.

A Slave to Debt

Only two days separate those who are living in prosperity and those who are not—yesterday and tomorrow. Prosperous people live on yesterday's money. Impoverished people live on tomorrow's money. Yesterday's money is your savings. Tomorrow's money is money you haven't got, so you borrow it from someone else.

The problem with borrowing money is that the people you borrow it from want it back plus a little extra for the privilege. That's why people who live on tomorrow's money become impoverished; tomorrow's money always costs more. The laws of compounding interest make tomorrow's money the most expensive money there is to use. Two days is not much. But once you have oriented yourself to living on tomorrow's money, it's a hard habit to break.

There is no law that says we must be in debt. We choose to borrow other people's money. It's easy to do because there is nothing but fun on the front end of the deal. But in doing so, we are buying very expensive money and putting ourselves into a position where it is difficult to ever get ahead. While there is nothing but fun on the front end of borrowing money, there is nothing but pain on the back end. We end up paying back two or three times as much as what we borrowed. Living on borrowed funds is not good prosperity behavior.

People can turn from heading to the poorhouse to heading for the 'freedomhouse' with one simple choice: "I will stop living on tomorrow's money and start living on yesterday's money." If yesterday's money is not enough to pay for today, you must scale back on today's spending.

Nothing rips you from the arms of prosperity as surely as incurring personal debts. Mary Hunt, respected authority on getting out of debt, says: "We pledge future income, yet unearned, for current expenses. Then it becomes next year's salary that will be required to pay for this year's expenses."

Admittedly, there is a mine field of credit opportunities waiting for us. Hardly a day passes in our household when we do not receive 'preapproved' loan and credit applications or phone calls offering such. Anyone with the slightest inclination towards debt would be hard pressed to resist the onslaught of loan offers.

Tracey is a young college graduate that I met some time ago. A talented girl with plenty of potential, she fell into the trap of using credit cards. Her initial reasons for using credit cards were understandable. Going through college was an easier process when there was a little extra cash around. Tracey saw her credit cards as an extra source of income.

Unfortunately, upon graduation she had become accustomed to the 'extra income' her credit cards were providing. Thus, she established a spending lifestyle that ended up putting her into slavery. Tracey tells her story in a letter that she wrote to me. The first part of her letter, reproduced here, highlights the hopelessness she felt.

My life was crazy and out of control. It was a vast sea of bad habits. I lived off my five credit cards. I was a slave to them, barely making the minimum payments each month. When I didn't have enough income to cover the minimum payments, I would work more or have a yard sale, whatever I had to do except stop spending. I would transfer balances from card to card with most of my payments going to pay interest. I had no hope of ever getting out of debt. I believed there was no way out so I just kept living that way.

By the time I came to you for help, I had accumulated a credit card debt of $13,000 and could no longer make the minimum payments because I had lost one of my extra jobs. You gave me hope by believing that I could escape the debt habit if I was willing to change. You gave me a reason to stop—telling me that there was a better way to live; a life that would not only benefit me but others as well.

I think the most important thing was that you saw the big picture when I was trapped by my shortsightedness. My life has always been one of quick fixes. That's why I would simply work more hours rather than change my spending habits. But step by step you have guided me into a permanent solution. The debt will be completely paid in fifteen months and my income will be double what it is now. You have helped me acquire the skills to manage my money and never return to the cards.

The final part of Tracey's letter, which I will share later, talks about the freedom that she is experiencing for the first time in years. When Tracey started living on credit, she had no idea of the final cost. Easy money had mutated into a debt that squeezed the happiness out of life.

On the news recently was the story of a man who was cleaning out the cage of his two hundred and seventy one pound python snake. He put the snake into his bathroom while he cleaned the cage. While in the bathroom, the snake wrapped itself around the toilet bowl and ripped it out of the floor. It then started on a seek and destroy mission, finally attacking his owner. The winner of this contest was going to be the last one breathing.

Fortunately, the owner was more attached to life than he was his snake. He had the snake prepared to become a neat pair of cowboy boots. Reflecting on his experience he said, "I never expected the snake to grow that large or to get that much out of hand." A lot of people who get into debt end up expressing the same sentiments: "I never expected the debt to grow that large and get that much out of hand."

For Freedom's Sake. . . Get out of Debt!

One of the people that I interviewed for this book was a consumer credit advisor. He told me of the most serious case of personal debt that he had encountered. A successful attorney, although good at law, was very bad at managing his money. Though his law practice earned him a high income, he still managed to accumulate four hundred and ninety-five thousand dollars in credit card debt. This was not including the debt he owed on his properties or leases on his vehicles! He needed Mr. Durham to administer some behavior modification!

The consumer credit advisor informed me of another interesting fact. Most of the people who came to him because of their financial troubles drove nicer cars than he did. He mused on this saying, "At least mine was paid for!"

If there is one thing that I want this book to teach you, it would be: Debt is the enemy of prosperity. You cannot have both debt and prosperity.

When Debt is Good

It's hard to make judgments on when debt is good. Some people have the spin of their personal experiences to show how debt has been a help to them. But on the whole, debt is much more likely to have a negative impact in the lives of those who incur it. It's much easier to draw conclusions about why debt is bad. When marriages break up and bankruptcies are declared as a result of debt, you draw the obvious conclusion.

Incurring personal debt for the sake of buying your house is acceptable. The price of a house is great and it is the biggest purchase most people make in their lifetime. There are two problems with saving up to pay cash for a house. First, you have to live somewhere while you are saving, and paying rent is a huge drag on your capacity to save. Second, the value of our savings can be eroded by inflation in the price of real estate.

Besides borrowing to buy a home, going into debt for the sake of buying a business or paying for vocational training could be acceptable. But for everything else, save up and pay cash.

Pay Off Your Home Loan Quickly

Be passionate in your efforts to work and to save in order to wipe out your home loan. Don't get seduced into thinking that just because the bank gives you a thirty year mortgage that you should take thirty years to pay it off. You'll be poor if you do. You are playing right into the bank's plan to make the most profit from you by stretching out your loan period.

If you cannot pay off a thirty year loan in fifteen years or less, you have bought too much house. Sure it might be a nice house but even a nice house ends up feeling like a ball and chain when you are still making payments on it decades later. Pay that mortgage down! You can do it if you decide to.

When Eleanor and I got married we were both students and had very limited resources.

My car was worth eight hundred dollars. It was my only real asset. I had just started an internship that paid modestly. To the marriage, Eleanor brought the assets of a study desk and a clock radio. She had a year of college left so it was some time before she was able to start earning an income. We had both received lots of love but no 'love gifts' from our parents.

Looking back, it was the best way to start. Though we had humble beginnings, we still managed to save and buy a one bedroom apartment. It was a fifteen year loan which we paid off in six years. We bought our next home with the help of a twenty year loan which we paid off in four years. The next home was a thirty year loan which we paid off in two years. The key? We make paying off our home mortgage a priority above other things.

Believe me, just because you get a thirty year home loan, it does not mean that you must take that long to pay it off. For those of you who live in countries where you can deduct the interest on your home loan against your taxable income, don't be seduced into not paying off your home loan. I will talk about this more in chapter eight. The tax deduction argument is not a good one. Owning your home free and clear is a key to experiencing prosperity.

Eliminate your Debting Ways

In the book *Master Your Money*, author Ron Blue writes: "Debt is never the real problem; it is only symptomatic of the real problem—impatience, poor self-image, lack of self-worth, lack of self-discipline, self-indulgence and greed." All of these negative traits make us prime targets for clever marketing, and for raising our spending every time we gain a raise in our income. Each one of us must examine why we are motivated to go into debt. The answer to our condition will be more accurately found by asking, "Why am I in debt?" not, "How did I get into debt?"

Putting on a wool sweater to keep you warm while swimming does not work. Likewise, putting on debt in order to gain freedom, time with the ones you love, success, wealth, self-esteem, personal fulfillment, inner peace, and fun does not work. To gain these things you must work at ridding yourself of personal debt. Whatever is the reason that motivated you to submerge your life beneath an ocean of debt, it is the enemy of your prosperity. You need to work out the reason why you are in debt and deal with it. Once you have owned up to the motivating factors that influence you to go into debt, enact this plan for getting back on top financially:

1) Stop spending now!
2) Set up a budget (spend less than you earn)
3) Sell, sell, sell to pay off debts
4) Start saving
5) Increase your income
6) Increase your savings

The best part about having a budget is that it frees you. As long as you are staying within your set limits, you can spend with peace of mind. A budget rescues you from guilty feelings.

Play Good Offense *and* Good Defense

How does a soccer team score ninety-eight goals in a game and still lose? Easy, if the opposing team scored ninety-nine goals. That is why you can have a huge income and still be enslaved by debt. It all depends on how much of your income you spend. Contrary to popular opinion, the secret to wealth is not in having a huge income. The world is filled with people who were once 'rolling in it' and who are now broke. How does it happen? Simple, the money that came in the front door went straight out the back door. They made it big and spent it big. In other words, they had a great offense but a weak defense.

To enter the world of prosperity, you must have a good earning to spending ratio. If you can keep a good portion of what you earn and invest it, then wealth is on its way. If you spend all that you make, you will never be prosperous. It is not so much what you make but how little of it you spend that's important. That's why a person earning twenty-nine thousand dollars a year can be wealthier than someone who earns ten times that amount.

The media trains us to think that becoming rich is the result of having a sensational wealth producing vehicle, for example, movie stardom, fame in the music industry, super athlete or super model status. All of these are sensational wealth producing vehicles. There is no denying that people with these vehicles can become very wealthy.

But it is wrong to think that unless you are in such a sensational vehicle you cannot be come wealthy. The truth is more millionaires are made out of ordinary people who wisely invest than Hollywood could ever produce. The ability to spend less than you earn and invest the difference is the only sensational thing a person needs in order to become prosperous.

No doubt it is good to work towards having a high income. But if all it does is lead to high spending, then you are no closer to prosperous living. Spending all that you earn simply saddles you with the burden of having to maintain that level of earning in order to keep your lifestyle.

Living in prosperity is having the lifestyle you want without ever worrying about keeping your job, surviving a recession or having a bout of illness. You cannot have a prosperous life if you let every dollar slip out the back door. Spending every dollar you earn, buys you a life of concern. You will always live with the nagging thought, "How will I survive if something untoward happens?" Living from paycheck to paycheck means being subject to the pain of every economic bump in the road.

You may be thinking, "Hey, it will be easier to save and invest when I start earning the big bucks." In reality, it will not be. The habits we create early in our lives usually dictate what we do later on. If you spend it all when you get a little, you will spend it all when you get a lot. Spending and saving are based on how much wisdom we have, not on how much income we have. Start feeling the prosperity coming to you. Spend less than you make and invest the difference.

Don't Be Tightfisted

Using a great defense to compliment one's offense can also be described as being frugal. Saving money by using it wisely and restraining one's spending are the characteristics of a frugal person. Being frugal has been deemed unfashionable these days, but it remains a key to becoming prosperous.

Don't, however, confuse being frugal with being tightfisted. Some people hold their money so tightly that they become painful to those around them. They always wait to see if someone else will pick up the bill before they offer to contribute. They are reluctant tippers. They are more comfortable with risking thousands on an investment than spending twelve dollars on a bunch of flowers. They are not skilled in the art of being thoughtful or generous.

Frugality never winces at paying its fair share and then some. A frugal spirit is not the enemy of a generous spirit. On the contrary, a prosperous person knows that giving money is the key to feeling like you have enough money. A tightfisted person does not realize that in being so resistant to letting money go, all they are doing is reinforcing the feeling that they never have enough.

Dave Ramsey, in his book *Financial Peace*, writes: "To think that the handling of your personal finances is merely a matter of math control is naive." Poverty is not just the result of having a lack of wealth. Poverty can also be the result of being tightfisted with the wealth you have.

The downside of developing an industrious propensity to save and invest is that you can become dominated by it. Being obsessed by a good habit is as bad as being trapped by a bad habit. Building a big financial barn and spending day and night contemplating how to fill it is an obsession. Such an obsession comes at the expense of building relationships.

Remember, money is more about mind control than math control. There is a huge difference between controlling your money and having it control you. Master it or become its slave. A tightfisted person is enslaved to keeping his or her money without regard to more important things in life.

Never let the acquisition of money lead you down the road of relational impoverishment. It is sad to see people accumulate vast wealth only to be bankrupt in relationships and dignity. I am reminded of the scene in the James Cameron movie *Titanic* when the wealthy Mr. Cal Hockley tried to buy himself a seat in a life boat. The ship's officer said, "Mr. Hockley, your money can't save you, any more than it can save me." With that, the ship's officer threw the money on to the deck of the sinking ship. People who relate more to money than to others, like the wealthy Mr. Hockley, are convinced that money can buy life. It is simply not that powerful.

Life is all about having wonderful relationships with people. Therefore, money is bad when the *lack* of it stops you from building relationships with people. It is just as bad when the *love* of it stops you from doing likewise. The tightwad prison is just as undignified as the spendthrift prison! Break free and move on to prosperity!

Quit Procrastinating with your Work

The art of procrastination has never made anyone prosperous. Putting off the work that needs to be done does nothing but delay your departure to prosperity. Procrastination is a potion made up of one part fear and one part laziness. It is a potion that we must stop drinking if we want to have a prosperous life.

At the end of the day, unless tainted with sickness, we must have produced more than we have spent. If not, we are spending too much or not working enough. Either way it's just a matter of time before we are making reservations at the Heartbreak Hotel.

I have developed a system to help keep my day focused on productivity. It's a simple clipboard system that holds a standard sheet of paper that has been specially designed as my 'daily task' record. Running down the left hand side are the numbers one through twenty-five. The opposite side of the page is reserved for taking down important notes from phone conversations. With the help of adhesive velcro, I have affixed a writing pen and a highlighter pen to my clipboard.

At the end of my day (or sometimes first thing in the morning), I sit down with my clipboard and list the tasks needing to be done for the coming day. As each task is accomplished, I take the highlighting pen and strike through the task. I carry my clipboard most everywhere I go when on the mission of completing the tasks. Any tasks not completed are carried forward to the next day's task sheet.

An eighty-nine cent clipboard may not be glamorous but it works. Sometimes I feel I must look like a football coach carrying my clipboard everywhere I go. But then again that is the spirit of what I am doing—coaching myself to better performance.

Whatever works for you, whether an exquisite leather-bound planner or a cheap clipboard, is acceptable. The important thing is to list out your tasks. This will hold you accountable for achieving what needs to be done. Procrastinating with your work delays the arrival of your prosperity.

Stop Procrastinating with your Bills

Most people who do not pay their bills on time do so for the following reasons. Either they do not have the money, they forget, or they want to make whoever is owed the money wait until the last minute for payment. Prosperity thinking does not operate this way.

Procrastination is an unbecoming habit, especially when it comes to fulfilling your financial obligations. I am not impressed by the person who brags about withholding due payments so that they can keep the money earning interest in their account for a few days longer. This behavior is the product of small thinking and prosperity is never produced by small thinking.

If you have incurred expenses, pay them! When you don't, the person who suffers the most is you because you have made your conditions unsuitable for the presence of prosperity. If you want prosperity, start behaving like a person of integrity. A simple way to feel your prosperity is to pay your bills on time.

Don't Steal Prosperity from Yourself

Have you ever been in a situation when you have been given more change than what was due in a transaction? I remember withdrawing some money from an automatic teller machine. I only requested forty dollars but the machine gave me eighty dollars. The receipt indicated a forty dollar withdrawal in the transaction, so nobody would have known had I pocketed the extra forty dollars as a tip from the bank. I was tempted but instead I went inside the bank and told the bank teller what had happened, thus handing over the extra forty dollars.

The bank teller accepted the money but looked at me quizzically as if I was crazy for not keeping it. I remember walking away thinking, "Well, they didn't seem that grateful, maybe I should have kept it." But prosperity reasoning prevailed. The loss at issue was not the bank's but mine. Had I kept the money, I would have been forty dollars richer and a little poorer in integrity.

Another time, I wasn't so quick to respond in the right way. I was at a fast food restaurant in Newport Beach. The service was tediously slow and very frustrating. Finally, getting my order, I noticed that they had mistakenly included an extra chocolate shake for which I had not paid. I thought about drawing their attention to the oversight but decided not to, justifying that it was the least they could do to compensate for keeping me waiting so long.

I drove away in the direction of the beach intent on enjoying my "free" chocolate shake but also feeling like I had just sabotaged a personal standard. Prosperity reasoning once again prevailed. I headed back to the restaurant, apologized and offered to pay for the drink. The girl serving at the counter brushed it off saying it wasn't a big deal and told me not to worry about it. But to me it was a big deal, and if not for their sake, certainly for my sake. I needed to make payment and she obliged. It was humiliating but the flavor of the shake was much better now that I had paid for it.

Prosperity cannot exist devoid of integrity.

Every time you act honestly, when nobody would know if you did otherwise, you prove that you are a person of integrity and prosperity.

Quit Quitting

Consider the words of Napoleon Hill: "No one is ever defeated until defeat has been accepted as a reality." As I wrote in my previous book, *Dating the Dream*: "Quitting may bring relief but it never brings reward." If you quit quitting, prosperity will naturally come to you.

Giving up on a mission is habit forming. The more you do it, the easier it is to do the next time. Before you know it, you have programmed yourself to be a quitter. It is a habit you must escape in order to experience prosperity in your life. Alter your course if you must, but never abandon your course just because it gets too hard.

I wrote a poem to help myself stay on course when the prevailing conditions make me feel like quitting. You may find it benefits you in such times.

Stay on Your Course

When things you confront do not go your way
That is basically how life is some days,
You can sulk and think you want to quit
Or decide you will just get over it.

You are only as big as what gets you down,
Your size is measured by what makes you frown,
The mind of a fool is the mind that gives in
To thinking that quitting will help you to win.

You have been here before you know from your past,
No profit is gained by giving up on the task,
Whatever you do problems always exist
But you know they give way to those who persist.

Take one step forward from your problem and find
That you have moved on and left your problem behind,
Say to the challenge, 'I'm bigger than you,'
When you stay on your course you prove that it's true.

Wes Beavis

Chapter 7

Escape from

Unproductive Situations

The tuna boat captain was pleased to have me join him for the trip. I was thrilled because the way my friend described commercial fishing made me think I was in for the most exciting day of my life. My friend said, "When the tuna strike, it's pandemonium. You can't hook 'em and pull 'em into the boat fast enough. You'll get so tired from slinging these huge fish over your shoulder, your arms will be killing you but you can't stop because of the excitement."

I couldn't wait. I had seen video footage of tuna fisherman whipping their industrial fishing rods back and forth like they were giving the sea a lashing. Each time they pulled their rods back, they would produce a snapping action that would pop the tuna right off the hook into the boat.

Just moments before the captain gave his orders to prepare to sail, I remembered that I had forgotten my sack lunch. I had, in the exciting rush to leave, left it on the kitchen counter where I was staying. Running as fast as I could while wearing rubber fishing boots, I retrieved my lunch and jumped into the forty foot tuna boat just as it was departing from the pier. The last thing I wanted was to be fifty miles out to sea with no food to replenish the energy that I was going to expend catching all those tuna.

The boat trip took us past the continental shelf where the ocean depth plummets. Once at that location, the captain slowed the boat down to 'trolling speed'. The first thing I noticed were the huge rolling waves. They slowly but methodically picked the boat up to crest the wave only to slump it down at the wave's base ten feet below. After an hour of unsuccessful trolling, I was feeling nauseous and decided that if the tuna were not biting, maybe I should have a bite myself. Going to my meal bag, I retrieved two sausage sandwiches smothered in ketchup. "This ought to settle my stomach," I thought.

Having nourished myself, I headed back onto the boat's rear deck to see if there was any action. I found nothing but bored fisherman telling stories of other times when the fish were biting. Then the wave hit me. No, not an ocean wave but the most ferocious wave of nausea.

The constant up and down motion of the boat coupled with a few sausage sandwiches became a lethal combination. For the next three hours, the only excitement on deck was me hurling my insides out. The sea captain thought it was funny and continued on his mission of tracking down the elusive tuna by trolling the ocean at 'hurl speed.' That night, we sailed into the harbor without so much as one fish for our efforts. About the only thing the day had produced was a world record in the number of times one could be sick.

Admittedly, it was just one unproductive day in the life of a fishing vessel, but that day symbolizes the lives of what many people face everyday. They spend lots of time going through the motions. They have plenty of ups and downs but at the end of the day, they don't bring home the tuna.

In order to experience prosperity in your life, you must escape unproductive situations. You have to release yourself from the things which do not contribute to your prosperity. Prosperity doesn't happen to us by accident. It comes to us because we have purposed our lives to achieving that end.

As I have already stated, prosperity does not need to be chased. It will come to you naturally when you escape the things that make you poor. You must desire prosperity, believe it is for you and then make it your goal. Otherwise you will have no reason to put in the effort to cause prosperity to come to you. On the other hand, if you can see that prosperity is right for you, then you will have great reason and motivation to escape the unproductive situations that hold you back from experiencing prosperity.

Here are twelve unproductive situations in which we can find ourselves. Conquer them.

1. A Poverty Mentality

As always, bringing about any outward change first starts with changing the way you think. You have to stop thinking that you are meant to struggle all your life. Rid yourself of the poverty thinking which you have bought into. Stop thinking that a life without 'tuna' is how life was meant to be.

For example, the other day a father was talking over with me the issue of whether paying rent or paying a mortgage was the best scenario for having a home. His conclusion was that there were pros and cons for both. I then posed a third scenario: "What about buying a home and paying it off. Then you have to pay neither rent nor a mortgage!" Staring back at me with a look of incredulity on his face and laughter in his voice, he said, "Yeah, like that could ever happen. Less than one percent of the population own their homes free and clear!"

Whether the accuracy of the one percent figure is right or not, it does not matter. He believed it in his mind and that made it truth for him. He has swallowed the idea that nobody owns their own home regardless of whether he has the ability to pay off a home or not.

Don't let the world's low standards and goals set yours. The world's thinking is geared to poverty principles not prosperity principles. Set your goals according to what your faith and potential can achieve, not according to what everybody else does.

2. A Boring Job

A job can enable us or it can hold us back from experiencing a better life. For too many a job is reduced to the 'penalty' one has to pay in order to have funds for living. This is not a situation where prosperity can flourish. Work is meant to be fulfilling and satisfying.

The problem many people encounter with their job is that their full potential is not utilized.

And when it comes to payment, the amount of the wage is often determined by what the job position pays, not necessarily what the person is worth.

An unsuitable job saps a person of self-worth and creative vitality. Unless it is seen as a stepping stone to something better, such a situation leads people to make decisions that further erode their prosperous potential.

Getting stuck in a job that underutilizes your talent and potential is unproductive and will hurt your prospects for prosperity. The only valid reason for you to have a boring job is if you are using the job as a stepping stone to something greater. People who have boring jobs are in a prime position to build personal businesses. Realize that the reason you are bored is that you have more to give than what the position asks of you. Therefore, instead of burning up your excess energy being frustrated and irritable, channel the energy into building your enterprise.

Always fulfill your duty to your job because integrity demands that we honor the ones who pay us with a fair day's work. But keep working towards the day when you can fulfill the real reason for your presence on the planet.

3. Playing Musical Ships

I like to picture my business as a ship that transports me to great places of prosperity. Being on board the business ship has been a tremendous help in escaping the things that could have made me poor.

There are many respected ships in the business fleet able to transport you to higher incomes. Climb aboard one and see where it can take you. Make sure it is one that suits you and has a proven track record in getting results. Then stick with the ship! Do not keep jumping ships, which so many people are prone to do, every time the seas get a little rough.

There is no such thing as a business that does not require hard work and perseverance. The only people who prosper from the 'easy, no effort required, once in a lifetime' money making opportunities are the ones who are selling them to you. Don't waste your time and energy chasing the easy way. Too many people jump from ship to ship in the vain hope of finding the 'magic one' that will give them what they want without effort. There is no such ship.

Stop playing musical ships. The answer is in sticking with your chosen vessel. If it was right for you in the first place, it will still be right for you even when the going gets hard. Bringing home the 'tuna' is inevitable as long as you stick with the ship long enough!

4. A Dull Marriage

A dull marriage repels the prosperity that a great marriage attracts. Making your marriage a good one is a super investment. Eleanor and I have been married for fourteen years. It started out as a wonderful marriage and it becomes better with each passing year.

We enjoy a great relationship because we invest in its well-being. One of the ways we do this is by having a date night every week. We have a standing arrangement with a sitter who watches our children while we go out on the town. Rarely do we allow anything to move in on this sacred territory. We plan for it and have come to cherish the blessing it has brought to our marriage.

I once asked a friend whether he still dated his wife. He replied, "Why chase a bus once you have caught it?" The reason is simple. Catching the bus is one thing, enjoying the journey is another!

In the first stage of a new romance, our responses to each other are charged with spine tingling sensations. As we become more secure with each other, the dynamics change. The relationship becomes deeper but it also becomes more predictable. We settle into comfortable patterns of behavior. We have kids, we get a dog and, before we know it, there's not much room for spontaneity. It leads to a condition that behavioral scientists call 'habituation.' Some refer to it as boring.

I once heard someone say, "Marriage is the closest thing to heaven or hell that you will experience on earth." Great marriages are made, they don't just happen. Put in the effort to keep it fresh, alive, romantic and invigorating. It takes just as much energy to endure a boring marriage as it does to sustain an exciting marriage.

If you are stuck in a lackluster marriage, get help. Sadly, by the time many couples seek help, too much foul water has passed under the bridge. Divorce is never good—just ask someone who has been through one. It devastates you personally, let alone what it does to you financially.

Prosperity tastes twice as good when it is shared with your lover and best friend. Make your relationship one that promotes rather than discourages prosperity in your life.

5. Being Outside of Your Gift Zone

There are some positions in life for which we are not wired up to succeed. We might, with the help of dogged determination, be able to function in the position adequately, but we will never excel. It is one thing to be out of our comfort zone, it is another thing entirely to be out of our gift zone. Occupying the wrong position in life, no matter how noble the position may be, is a waste of your life. If it always feels foreign and seems out of step with the way you are wired up to function, it is an unproductive situation. It merely delays you from doing that which will release you to prosper.

6. Being Seduced by Planned Obsolescence

Back in 1929, General Motors executive Floyd Allen said: "Advertising is in the business of making people helpfully dissatisfied with what they have in favor of something better. The old factors of wear and tear can no longer be depended upon to create a demand. They are too slow." Thus, as early as the 1920's, Detroit began pioneering the concept of the annual model change and it has not stopped since.

We throw a lot of investment money out of the window when we feed the need to constantly update to the latest model.

Yes, take advantage of new innovations, but don't give in to the feeling that you always have to have the 'latest'. At the rate products get superseded, you can skip every second or third new model, buy the fourth and get all the previous innovations included. Meanwhile, if you are investing the money that you would have used to 'update', you are way ahead. Being a captive to planned obsolescence will keep you broke.

7. Driving Away without your Freedom

The day I passed my driver's test and was duly ordained as a moving vehicle operator was a thrilling one. My first solo drive was along a stretch of highway that followed the ocean coastline for miles. Driving the open road, in charge of my geographical destiny, was the greatest feeling of freedom.

This newly discovered freedom, however, came at the expense of something else—my financial freedom. A sizeable portion of my income was now committed to repaying the money I had borrowed to purchase a 1972 Leyland Marina. Though reviewed by *Wheels Magazine* as a sedan that "handled well at parking speeds," I justified my purchase to be worthy of the imposition of monthly repayments.

It is easy to justify the purchase of a vehicle. It is just as easy to finance the purchase. This can be hazardous territory in our drive to prosperity. When financing a vehicle on credit, you may drive away in a new car but in doing so, you leave some of your freedom behind. In essence, you invite an entity into your life to take regular bites out of the fruit of your labor. Furthermore, with vehicle leases, this controlling entity puts restrictions on how many miles you can drive per year before being penalized.

Driving a vehicle that is safe and reliable is important. However, justifying a loan or lease by thinking, 'It is better for business if I drive something that makes me look successful,' is dubious. The notion that driving a nice car will attract success causes many to finance expensive vehicles which they otherwise, could not afford.

Buying a fancy car is not the key to building a business. The reality is that hard work, getting clients, building relationships, and making sales is the key to success. A stylish car will not cause clients to automatically start calling you. In your efforts to drive something that represents your business, be careful that you do not heap upon yourself another financial pressure.

Remember, prosperity is calculated by your freedom. Drive a car that you own. This way you are free from monthly repayments and, in the case of a lease agreements, free from anyone telling you how many miles per year you are allowed to drive.

8. The New Television

The biggest terminator of people's productivity up to now has been the television. But a new television has come to town—the internet. This 'new' television is even more subtle in the way that it can hook you because there is 'so much helpful information on the world wide web!'

Both the internet and television have their place in our lives. There are fine qualities that can be found with both mediums, but they still have a huge capacity to waste our time. By all means use the internet. But recognize that your excesses will delay the arrival of a prosperous life.

9. Accumulating Junk

How many people leave their cars parked on the street because their garage is full of junk that isn't worth a fraction of what their car is worth? Get rid of your junk and stop accumulating it. You do not have wealth because you keep buying stuff. And stuff is the stuff that ties you down and takes away your sense of being free.

10. Neglecting Your Health

There is nothing quite as heartwrenching as having plenty of friends, time and money but not having the physical capability to enjoy them. This is one area where life can give us less than what we deserve. Some good people are imprisoned with ailments even though they have been wise in taking care of themselves.

However, to those blessed with good health, it is essential to eat nutritious meals, exercise and get regular health checks. We have no idea what the future holds for us healthwise. But we can increase our potential to live extended healthy lives. Ask yourself the question: "What is likely to happen to me if I live on pepperoni pizza and watch sports on television for exercise?"

Neglecting your health is an unproductive situation. Examining the consequences of neglecting our bodies makes us aware of the need to change our oil regularly. Remember, we may be lucky enough to get a new spark plug but full engine replacement is another story.

11. Pornography

Do not indulge yourself with pornography. Why? Simply because it is a form of fun that does not end with fun. It is addictive and, over time, will erode your ability to be satisfied with your partner. It leads to loneliness—the opposite of prosperity.

12. Co-signing

This is a very unproductive situation in which to become involved. Basically, co-signing is assuring a financial institution that you will pay the debt incurred by another if they default on their repayments. I almost learned this the hard way. A good friend of mine asked me if I would co-sign on a loan. He said that his mother was ill and needed the money to help with her expenses. It seemed like a noble reason and my friend had a honorable reputation in the community. The loan was for twenty thousand dollars.

One day I got home from work to receive a letter from the bank telling me that my friend had defaulted on his payments. The bank's letter stated it was now time for me to 'step up to the plate' in his stead. Fortunately, I was able to get the problem resolved. Years later it was discovered that my friend had a gambling addiction that devastated his marriage, his family, the community and his financial future. Never co-sign for anybody unless you are willing to lose both the money and the relationship. For one goes with the other.

Gordon Powell in his book *Happiness is a Habit* says, "Pruning is necessary. To get the most out of life you have to cut things out." If you believe that prosperity is for you, then start pruning. Get out the big clippers of life, oil them up, and start to cut the unproductive situations out of your life. I have mentioned a few in this chapter. Of course, some of these may apply to you while others may not. In reality, you know what areas of your life are holding you back. Prosperity awaits the person who prunes their life to create space for more productive situations. Chop, chop. Ching! Ching!

Chapter 8

Escape from the
Grip of Taxes

How would you like to never have to worry about taxes again? It is possible. There is a way available to us. We can sleep peacefully every night in the knowledge that we are no longer burdened by taxes. This secret is known by some, yet there are many more who should be enjoying this freedom. This 'escape' is not limited to people living in a certain country, or class, or income bracket. Whoever you are, you can be free from the grip of taxes forever.

How? Pay your taxes.

That's right! Render unto Caesar what is Caesar's. "What? That's no revolution," you say.

You are correct. When it comes to taxation, there is no revolution. With success comes tax. You will pay it. If abiding by the laws of the land means anything, you have no choice apart from using your voting power to change government policy. Accept it and get over it. This is the bad news.

But harken now for the good news. Though you cannot escape paying some tax as you succeed, you can escape the grip that taxes can have on your spirit. You cannot evade taxes but you can evade the anxiety of what tax responsibilities can do to you.

Ever since I have known him, a friend of mine has complained about the taxes that he pays. After not seeing him for five years, I finally met up with him again. I couldn't believe my ears. Within twenty minutes, he was back to griping about the government's heavy hand of tax. Of all the positive things we could have been talking about, he defaulted to this subject.

The first step to releasing the grip of taxes on your life is to accept the inevitability of tax. If you are successful, you will pay tax and the greater your success, the greater your taxes will be. Accept it and call it your association dues for living in a country with great amenities.

Employ the Government

As I wrote out the check for twenty-six thousand dollars in favor of the tax office, I should have been more depressed. In the time leading up to this check writing occasion, however, I had done some soul searching. My initial thoughts were begrudging ones. I did not agree with quite a few of the government's decisions and regretted seeing my hard earned tax dollars supporting such policies. Thinking this way did not make the process any easier.

Then I started thinking about the government funded projects that I appreciated: schools, teachers, roads, law enforcement, hospitals, clean water supply, and national security. As I wrote out my check, I imagined the money going to these noble causes. It felt good to think that I was paying a good share of a teacher's annual salary, it felt good to think that I was paying for the training of some police officers and it felt good to think that I was helping a hospital to save some lives.

There was nothing I could do to change the fact that the check had to be written. But what I could change was how I saw the funds being used. In my mind, I was no longer paying taxes. Rather, I was employing the government to do some great things. Take this view when you pay your taxes and feel the grip loosen.

There's No Such Thing as a Tax Problem

All of what you earn is not all of yours to spend. A certain portion must be set aside for your tax obligations. People only have a tax problem when they spend this portion. Groan about it all you want, but the tax man shows no compassion when it comes to wanting his share. Spare yourself the sleepless nights. There's nothing quite like the peace one has in knowing that the funds are there ready for the tax man when he knocks. It is another great way to escape the grip of taxes.

Know the Truth about Tax Deductions

Do not let the lure of a tax deduction keep you from becoming prosperous. Some people are so averse to paying tax that they incur high tax-deductible debt or they spend all their money on tax-deductible items just to avoid paying a few dollars in tax. There is nothing wrong or illegal about this intention. However, they are reducing their prospects of experiencing prosperity.

Be discerning in how much value you place in tax deductions. With a few exceptions, there is no such thing as a free tax deduction. In order to save a few percent in taxes, we can end up having to spend the balance on items which do not contribute to our wealth. It would be better to pay the tax and put the balance into income producing investments.

In some countries, the tax laws allow the interest on one's home to be tax-deductible. While this can be a good perk, it often has the reverse effect. It encourages people to keep a high level of debt on their homes. Studies have shown that in the long run, you are better to pay off your home as quickly as possible. Yes, you will lose the tax deduction and yes, you will have to pay some extra taxes. But these benefits far outweigh any losses.

First, you will experience the joy of what it is to own your home. Second, you will no longer be paying a huge mortgage payment which releases money to pay your taxes. Third, in most cases, there will be so much left over after paying taxes that you can start investing like a millionaire because you are on your way to becoming one.

The tax deduction that is an undeniable winner is a tax deferred retirement account. It is an allowance whereby you can invest pre-tax dollars into an account that is redeemable after a certain age. Contributing to a tax-deferred retirement account means that you get every dollar of your contribution back plus most of your interest. Depending on your government's regulations, there are limits on how much you can contribute in any given year. However, this should be the first investment opportunity of which you should take advantage.

Keep Your Accounting Simple

There is little nobility in paying more tax than you are required. A tactical and trustworthy accountant can help you find ways to minimize the amount of tax you have to pay. Take advantage of the allowances but do yourself a favor and keep your tax accounting simple.

Some tax minimization plans embroil you in such complex bookkeeping that it becomes difficult to administrate and understand. The savings that any complex plan may achieve could be eroded by the extra fees and administrative demands. Keeping your accounting as simple as possible will bring you more peace of mind and make Caesar less suspicious.

They Can't Take it All

Remember, regardless of how much you earn, the tax department cannot take it all from you. At worst, they can take half. And, at that, the more of your half you give away to tax-deductible charities, the more the tax department has to give their half back to you. And as someone once remarked, until the tax rate is one hundred percent it is always better to make a dollar than to not make a dollar. Don't live under the grip of taxes any longer. No one needs to have the plans for prosperity foiled because of taxation.

Chapter 9

Escape from

Anxiety and Worry

In his book *Strength for Today*, John MacArthur relates the following story. During World War II, the death of many adults left many orphaned children. At the close of the war, the Allies provided camps to feed and keep the orphans until new homes for the children were found. The children were treated with the finest of food and care. In one of the camps, however, the officials were perplexed because the children could not sleep. They would eat three good meals during the day but at night, they would lie awake. The camp authorities brought in some doctors to study the situation.

The doctors provided a solution. Every night when the little children were put to bed, someone would come down the row of beds and place in each little hand a piece of bread. So the last thing the children experienced at night was grasping a piece of bread. In a matter of days, they were all sleeping through the night. Why? Even though they were fed sufficiently during the day, experience had taught them that there was no hope for tomorrow. When they had the bread tucked in their hands, they knew that they would at least have breakfast the next day.

Many people have the same anxiety when it comes to their finances. They feel the most secure when they have a paycheck in their hands. It tells them that for the next few days, while the money lasts, everything will be okay. Yet, as always, the money does run out and usually before someone tucks another paycheck or commission in their hands. They are left with little choice than to get used to this tide of security coming in for a few days and then departing when the money runs out.

The hardest reality is that we live in an age when job security is no longer assured. The greatest concern about living from paycheck to paycheck is what happens if the tide goes out and stays out for a while. For example, what if you lose your secure job. Many studies have shown that the average family is only one pay-check away from financial disaster.

A few years ago, when Eleanor and I immi-grated to the United States, we brought with us a significant sum of money in the form of U.S. bank drafts. One of the first tasks upon arrival was to go to the bank and open an account into which we could deposit the drafts and start making withdrawals. Our plans were thwarted. The bank official told us that since we were new residents to the area, we would have to wait three weeks before they would clear the funds and make them available to us.

We only possessed a few dollars in U.S. currency so we found ourselves in the position of having to make it last for three weeks. We decided to buy groceries with the funds that we had so that at least there would be food in the house. We shopped for what we needed and proceeded to the cashier. As the amount was totalled, Eleanor reached into her pocket to retrieve some cash we had set aside. To our horror, we discovered that the money was miss-ing. Eleanor, who was battling a sinus infection at the time, concluded that the process of retrieving a tissue from her pocket several times during the shopping expedition must have resulted in the money falling out. We searched up and down the shopping aisles to no avail. The money was gone and in its place was a sense of dread and misery.

Though the experience caused us some despair, at least it was short lived. In three weeks, the bank cleared our funds and we were back in business. It was just a little taste of the pressure that many people live with constantly; the worry and anxiety of how they are going to make it from one week to the next.

When you are just starting out, you do tend to live from paycheck to paycheck. But if you employ the principles of prosperity, you can move through this stage quickly. No one needs to be stuck in a hand-to-mouth existence forever. By engaging the prosperity principles to your resources, even if they are limited, you can be in a position of living without anxiety about money.

A Life of Fewer Bills

The quality of your life goes up when the number of monthly bills go down. Bills are a drag on the human spirit. Get rid of them. Your sense of personal freedom will soar when you reduce the amount of monthly accounts you have to pay.

There are three ways to get rid of the bills in your life. First, stop handing out invitations for people to bill you. Examine all the monthly accounts that get mailed to you and ask yourself whether you really need that service the biller is providing. Sure, the service may not cost that much but when you add the bills together and multiply them over a year, it works out to be a huge chunk of your income.

One of the reasons I do not have cable television is that I want one less entity in my life laying claim to my income. Cable television is great and doesn't cost that much. But I have discovered that my quality of life increases with fewer bills rather than more television channels.

The second way to reduce the bills in your life is to pay off your debts. Every one of them. You say, "But Wes, that's impossible!" Yes, if you think becoming debt free is impossible then you will never be debt free. But if you believe that it is possible and put in the effort required you will succeed in the quest. Experience the thrill. Savor the satisfaction of living without the worry of owing people money.

Third, pay cash for everything. If you don't have the money, do not buy it. Delay your gratification. A friend of mine says, "Better to have it one day late than one day early." There is much more satisfaction in paying your way through life with cash.

Life is more peaceful when you live on cash rather than live on credit. No longer do you have to deal with the guilt of a purchasing something that you have not earned. I am not saying never use a credit card. What I am saying is never use a credit card *if* you haven't got the money already sitting in your bank account to cover the charge. It takes discipline but by now, you should have discovered that discipline makes you successful.

Never Fear a Rainy Day

Our ancestors established the practice of saving for a rainy day. In the modern age, we have deemed this practice unnecessary. A credit card could always be our savior in the event of a rainy day. However, we have begun to use the credit card as a way of adding extra enjoyment to our sunny days. Now, instead of it being our helper in the event of a rainy day, it has become a source of bad economic weather itself. What has eventuated is that most people do not have the resources to sustain them in the event of a moderately cloudy day, let alone a rainy one.

Many financial advisors recommend having six months of living expenses saved in order to provide a cushion if the 'unexpected' were to occur. Having a cushion is a great way to relieve you of worrying about how you would survive if something unexpected happened. Of course, the fewer debts you have, the longer you can live on your cushion.

Do not be misled by thinking that a rainy

day fund is a sign of pessimism or lack of faith. Houses are built to be watertight because we know that sometimes storms do come. Yet nobody would accuse home builders of being pessimistic or showing a lack of faith. Why should it be any different when it comes to our money management? Rainy days are inevitable. In reality, those who have a savings cushion can be the most positive because they can sail through bad times without having the burden of wondering how they are going to survive.

Having rainy day savings brings the sunshine back into a stormy situation. Having a water resistant financial house brings peace of mind.

Never Fear Losing Your Job

One of the great blessings of living prosperously is that you never have to fear losing your job. What is more, living without the fear of losing your job actually enables you to perform better. The net result is that you are more likely to keep your job for as long as you want.

People who have high levels of debt and no savings are more likely to make desperate decisions in the face of job upheavals. They are more likely to accept cuts in pay, benefits or position because they know the prospects of being without a job for a few weeks could cripple them. Prosperous people have more serenity and much less desperation in the face of unexpected upheavals. Because of their savings and low levels of debt, they can take the time to pursue the *best* solution not just the *first* solution.

More Peace as a Parent

Few things do more to reduce our anxiety than the knowledge that the future of our children is secure. How do we achieve this? How much money do we need to give our kids in order to ensure their success and survival? Not one dollar! In fact, studies have conclusively shown the more money you give your children, the more you rob them of their own prosperity.

Never give money to your children until they are successful enough not to need it. This seems to be such a contradiction to what we feel is right. Shouldn't our children be the recipients of our money as a sign of our love? It seems a noble act of kindness but it is wrong.

Our giving actually robs them of something

163

much greater. It robs them of their development in economic productivity. In other words, if we keep giving them our resources then they will never have the need to produce their own resources.

The authors of *The Millionaire Next Door* pose this question and then provide the answer: "What can you give your children to enhance the probability that they will become economically productive adults? In addition to an education, create an environment that honors independent thoughts and deeds, cherishes individual achievements, and rewards responsibility and achievement."

I have learned much about this subject from a good friend named Steve and how he deals with his own three sons. Steve is an established and successful entertainer who tours extensively and always brings at least one son with him on tour. On one occasion, my performing schedule enabled Steve and I to join together for a concert. During the concert, Steve's six year old son Jordan came on to stage with his own electric guitar. It was not a toy guitar but a miniature version of the real thing. For the next few songs, Jordan was on stage belting out songs with his dad, strumming his electric guitar with all the moves of a country rock star.

After the concert, I was telling Steve how great it was to have his son a part of his performance. Steve went on to tell me how it had been Jordan's idea. He wanted to buy his own guitar and start performing with his dad. Steve could have bought the guitar for Jordan to enable him to do so but he didn't. Instead, he told Jordan that if he wanted a guitar he would have to earn the money to buy one.

Jordan thought about it and came up with the idea that he could draw pictures, sign them, and sell the pictures at his dad's concerts for fifty cents each. At every concert, Steve would be signing albums and Jordan would be signing pictures that he had drawn. At the end of one concert tour, Jordan had sold enough drawings to buy his guitar.

Observing Steve teach his sons in this way inspired me. Since then, I have been deliberate in my efforts to teach my sons about free enterprise and productivity. Whenever they want to buy something, rather than ask for the money, they ask for a job. Once the job is completed, I pay them. Part of the training is that, upon receiving payment, they must firmly shake my hand, make good eye contact and say, "Thank you for your business."

I recently heard Dr. Robert Schuller say,

"The pride of earnership is much greater than the pride of ownership." It is true. You know it based on the experience of your own life. And it is the pride of earnership rather than money which is the more valuable thing you can give to your child.

Our children and our money are two of the most critical areas of our lives. It is one of life's perplexing mysteries that neither of them come with an instruction manual. We know that there is no magic formula guarantee of success with either. But the principles of prosperity will increase our potential to have less worry and more success with both.

Chapter 10

Escape to

The Prosperous Life

From across my office table, I could see the tears in Megan's eyes. Fortunately, they were a sign of her relief and joy rather than tears of sorrow.

Thirty minutes before, Megan had come to me seeking some financial advice. Megan and her husband had been considering whether a lease or a bank loan would be the better financial arrangement in buying a new car. I asked her how much money they currently owed. She answered, "We don't owe anything."

I felt she had misunderstood my question

so I asked her again, this time being more specific about outstanding credit card balances and current car loans. Megan replied, "That's just it. We cut up our credit cards ten years ago and we own the cars that we drive. We don't owe any money to anybody." I then posed the question: "Why do you want to start borrowing now?"

Megan told me that her teenage son was starting to get embarrassed about having mom drive him around in such an old car. "It is an old car," Megan agreed, "but it runs great and never gives us any trouble. When I start to feel down about it being an old car, I get out there and give it a good clean. It seems to restore my pride in driving it."

Not being able to contain myself, I said, "Megan, let your son be embarrassed. It will deepen his character!" As we continued talking, Megan shared how her family dreamed of driving a big red truck. I told her that one day she and her husband could pay cash for that truck. We worked out a plan whereby they could continue to live their peaceful life of no debts as well as have their red truck some time in the future.

Then I spent the next twenty minutes pouring on the praise. I told Megan how proud I was of her and her husband for not 'giving in' to the debt trap. I told her that their commitment to living debt free has put them on a course to becoming very wealthy.

What brought tears to her eyes was hearing someone honor them for choosing to live a life without debt. They had felt very alone in their commitment to this lifestyle.

Megan told her son that his parents would not be putting the family under financial pressure for the sake of having a new vehicle. Her son not only understood, but said that he was proud to have parents who take such a radical stand.

I look forward to the day when I will see Megan's family driving a red truck. It may be a while, but until then, I know they are one less family living under the stress of financial pressures. They have a moderate income, but they are living with more prosperity than many families who earn much more.

Within our street is a wonderful lady who runs a day care center in her home. Each day, a parent drives up in an exquisite BMW and drops off a beautiful two year old daughter. Ten hours later, the BMW returns to transport the child back home. Five days a week, the two year old girl is in the care of someone other than her parents. Something is wrong with this picture.

There is nothing wrong with a fine BMW and the lifestyle that it accompanies, unless, in the process of having it, you or someone else becomes impoverished. Should our children pay for our immediate gratification any longer?

Let's quit 'enjoying it now and paying for it later.' Rather, let's have the good life for all our lives. It is possible if we stop putting holes in the bottom of our boat. It is time for us to get prosperity minded in our approach to life.

Being prosperity minded is more than just a money thing. The reason why this book has particularly focused on money is because it's often the doorway through which prosperity flows in and out. Money invades every important area of our lives. Therefore, the way we handle our money has an effect upon every area of our life. Handle it well and our whole life benefits. Handle it poorly and our whole life struggles.

In chapter six, I shared the letter from Tracey who had every part of her life affected by crippling debt. As soon as she broke free from the credit lifestyle, prosperity started to flow into all areas of her life. Tracey describes the freedom in the final part of her letter:

At least three incredible blessings have come from this new freedom. One is that I am able to enjoy my work for its own sake, not just as a means to supporting my addictive credit habit. I now enjoy my work like I could never before.

I have been able to give to good causes which has brought peace to my life. Before, I would write checks only to tear them up so that I could use the funds to pay the interest on my debts. And I have new hope for the future, that I will be able to enjoy the blessings that God gives me, and encourage others who are struggling with what I battled.

Abusing credit cards was a ridiculous way to live and a waste of the resources that I had. Who knows how long it would have taken to pay off that debt without your help? I am serious when I say that you have saved my life.

You don't quite realize the weight of the things that make you poor until from beneath their pressure, you break free. Prosperity begins with breaking free from the things that cripple your spirit. Whether that be your low self-opinion, the effect of your imperfections, the influence of depreciating people, poverty thinking, your spending habits, basically, whatever introduces the struggle into your life. Prosperity will come to you when you break free from these things.

171

And prosperity will come in the form of the following:

- Self-fulfillment
- Financial victory
- Personal freedom

That is what *Escape to Prosperity* is all about. Liberating you to have more of what brings you lasting satisfaction and joy.

Prosperous Living

Imagine yourself in this situation. The next time you receive a call from a finance company offering to consolidate all your debts into one monthly payment, being able to say, "I really appreciate your offer but I have no debts."

Imagine yourself being in a situation when you never have to ask or apply for vacation time. You simply say to your family, "Let's get out of here for a while!"

Visualize yourself being free to give your attention to fulfilling your dreams. Think about what high road you could take knowing that the needs of the low road are covered.

One of my favorite proverbs is: "A generous

man will prosper. He who refreshes others will himself be refreshed." Can you imagine the refreshment you are going to feel in life because your freedom has enabled you to be generous? Picture yourself giving thousands of dollars to worthy causes.

I am not saying the prosperous life is a perfect life. There will always be challenges in life. Yet, experience has convinced me that challenges are better faced from a position of prosperity than from a state of struggling. A person living in abundance knows the truth in the old saying: "When prosperity arrives, weakness is decreased."

Don't settle for mere survival. Living a life of constant struggle is a blight against your design and saps you of vitality. You are meant to live way above survival. You have an amazing creative potential that is meant to be explored. Being prosperous releases you to explore your creative potential and helps you to discover the true purpose for your existence.

Do not be seduced any longer by the things of this world that keep you poor. Experience the fulfillment of a liberated life. Let your abundance lead to further abundance. Savor the quality of your life as you are reminded again and again of how good it feels to be free and more able to give.

Deliberately plan to be prosperous. Dream of yourself having more than you need. Apply the prosperity principles and experience the thriving quality of life that you desire.

Other books by Wes Beavis

Become the Person You Dream of Being

176 pages
US$10.95

Dating The Dream

Building a Winning Relationship with Your Desires

192 pages
US$10.95

To order call:
(Toll Free) 1-877-WES-BOOK
or go to: www.WesBeavis.com
or fax: (413)825-8137

POWERBORN
631 Via Paraiso
Corona, CA USA 92882